GHOSTS OF MADISON, INDIANA

I0805718

GHOSTS OF MADISON, INDIANA

VIRGINIA DYER JORGENSEN

Haunted America

Published by Haunted America
A Division of The History Press
Charleston, SC 29403
www.historypress.net

Copyright © 2012 by Virginia Dyer Jorgensen
All rights reserved

All photos taken by author.

First published 2012
Second printing 2015

Manufactured in the United States

ISBN 978.1.60949.744.6

Library of Congress Cataloging-in-Publication Data

Jorgensen, Virginia Dyer.
Ghosts of Madison, Indiana / Virginia Dyer Jorgensen.
p. cm.
Includes bibliographical references.
ISBN 978-1-60949-744-6
1. Ghosts--Indiana--Madison. 2. Haunted places--Indiana--Madison. I. Title.
BF1472.U6J68 2013
133.109772'13--dc23
2012034053

Notice: The information in this book is true and complete to the best of our knowledge. It is offered without guarantee on the part of the author or The History Press. The author and The History Press disclaim all liability in connection with the use of this book.

All rights reserved. No part of this book may be reproduced or transmitted in any form whatsoever without prior written permission from the publisher except in the case of brief quotations embodied in critical articles and reviews.

Dedicated to those who keep an open mind about the other side.

CONTENTS

ACKNOWLEDGEMENTS

I am fortunate to know so many wonderful people who have generously given their time and talents to help me with this endeavor. It has always been my pleasure to tell as many people as I can about the infinite assets of the beautiful city of Madison. It is a wondrous city, and I am happy to live here.

There are many who generously assisted me in Madison in various capacities: Janice Barnes, Mike Totten, Bill and Betty Murphy, Gerry Reilly, Nathaniel Montoya, Camille Fife, Jan Vethrus, Libby Mann, Vickie Young, Corinna Davis, Link Ludington, Ben and Laurle Clemens, Ellie Smith, Ron Grimes, Jacquie Grimes, Dirk Cheatham, Elizabeth Buchanan and Polly O'Connor.

There are also many whom I would also like to thank who are not in Madison but whose abilities greatly assisted the creation of this book. I have gained two dear friends during this project: Barbie Guitard Canipe, whose artistic talents found numerous outlets, helped me navigate the publishing procedures, made graphic enhancements to some of the ghostly photographs along with the artist photo and gave advice born of a creative mind and a kind heart, and Mary Middleton Miller, who generously assisted with the formatting of the images. My commissioning editor Joe Gartrell and Jill Beitz of Indianapolis were also quite helpful. A long-awaited thank-you goes to Cindy Bobinac; Charmaine Gardner; my sister, Linda Dyer Smith; and my children, Brett, Lacy and Dustin, for their encouragement to write *Ghosts of Madison, Indiana*.

I must thank my mother, who inspired my love of reading, and my father, for his kind wisdom.

Mostly, I want to thank my husband, Dennis, who puts up with all my crazy schedules, meetings and career choices. He has encouraged me in every project that I have ever undertaken, no matter how impossible it seemed, and always said, "You can do it." It was no different with this project.

And of course, I thank the heavenly spirit, who is ever present and helps to guide my hand.

INTRODUCTION

Now are thoughts thou shalt not banish,
Now are visions ne'er to vanish;
From thy spirit shall they pass
No more, like dew-drop from the grass.
—Edgar Allan Poe

It is a little-known fact that Madison may well be one of the most haunted towns in America. It has the setting where you would expect to find spirits—a good long history and 133 blocks of original period buildings. Some who live here may not want that detail to be revealed. They want to move forward and leave the past behind. But there are some spirits who will not go along with being left behind.

Madison, Indiana, on the "great bend" of the Ohio River, claims the year 1809 as the date of its founding. At more than two hundred years old, it has enjoyed its share of history. Even before the town was settled, it had been a popular Indian camp and crossing for hundreds of years. A few hearty souls built rough cabins in the area before investors bought up large tracks for development. Madison's location on the river supported its prolific growth, and by 1850, it was the largest city in the state of Indiana. A booming economy encouraged the construction of beautiful homes by successful businessmen. Many of the wonderful buildings from Madison's early times are still standing and being used as homes, businesses and museums.

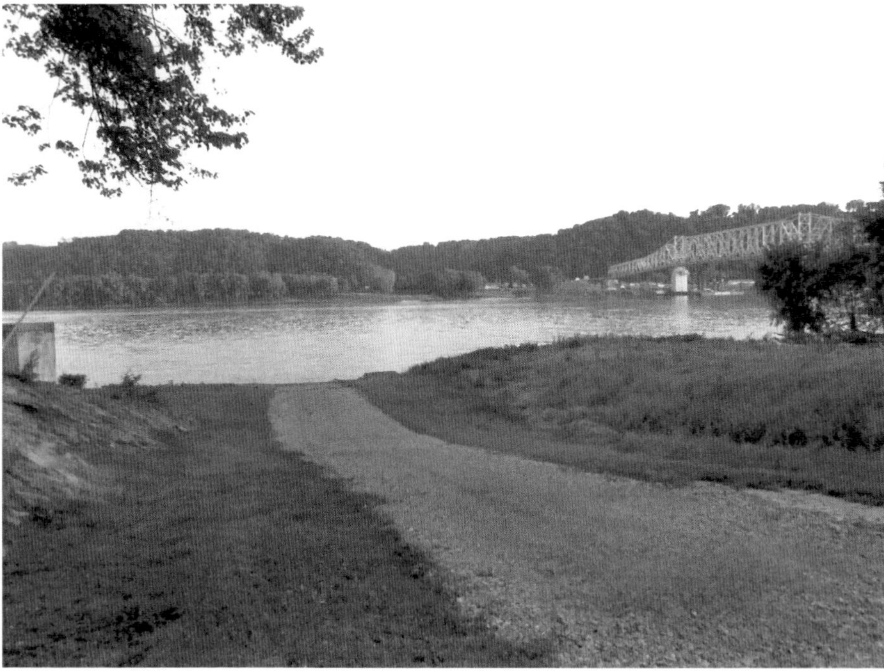

One hundred years ago, this area was the site of the Madison ferry landing, a scene of much shipping activity at the base of Ferry Street on the Ohio River.

The beauty of Madison draws many to visit and many to settle here until the inevitable rest that takes us all. Those who have lived and died here have formed an attachment to this area that rests between the Ohio River and the hills of North Madison. Tourists love to visit the charming Landmark Historic District; however, most don't realize that the past is much more alive than they would ever suspect. Places that have been settled for a long time, and where many lives have been lived, invariably have some spirits who for some reason do not move on. Instead they linger, pestering the living with their antics.

Perhaps you don't believe in ghosts. Lots of people who have come to Madison didn't believe before they came here, either. But read on about a few of the encounters of residents. There are many more stories not reported in these pages, but the residents will be glad to tell you themselves.

These spirits have been heard and seen in many of the old structures of Madison. Some of them seem to want for us to know that they are there. Others have stayed behind to repeat over and over some action that occurred during their living days. You may catch them going about their tasks, unaware that it was finished long ago. Whether they were taken too soon, had ends that were sudden or violent or passed quietly after long lives, for some reason the natural transition to rest in peace was not fulfilled. In those cases, the soul is caught between their time as living beings and their place in the next world.

Your paranormal experience may consist of hearing someone walking along a wooden floor, down a hallway or in a room above you; people talking or whispering in the corners; or traces of stale cigarette or cigar smoke or the scent of perfume lingering in the air. All of these tell you that you are not alone. Full-out encounters may encompass seeing red glowing eyes, a floating face or a full-body apparition. You may even feel a shove or have objects hurled at you. They may completely ignore you—as if *you* are the one who is not there—or they may try to interact with you, a feeling that most of us find very unexpected and uncomfortable if not downright frightening.

The stories here are all true accounts of paranormal experiences. How you view spiritual matters will influence how you receive them. It may just be a book about the history of Madison, with events that are relatively unheard of. We can contemplate the spirits' identities from their living days, as well as the possibilities for why they have not moved on. As for some, they are lost to history, and we may never know who they were.

Some of the spirits featured in the stories are located in private homes, so treat and respect them as such. Please do not knock on the door and ask for a tour of their home. Some are open to the public. You can visit or stay at several of the places described in these pages. When you are staying in the rooms where the spirits dwell, you may recall the stories of others' experiences and look around wondering if you will see what they have seen. While walking down the streets, you may feel the hair on your arm raise or a tug on your sleeve or hear whispering behind you when no one is there. You are just enjoying some of the local essence that the residents of Madison experience quite frequently.

What Do Ghosts Want and Why Are They Here?

We don't see things as they are, we see them as we are.
—Anaïs Nin

Ghosts are real, but they are unreliable. You can't make an appointment with them or call them and expect them to show up. They even mislead some of the ones who are intuitive to their thoughts. They give readings based on what they see in their realm, in their reality, based on what they know. Our reaction to them is based on our feelings about seeing an unexpected apparition and how much we know about spiritual subjects.

They use tricks to fool us and sometimes fool themselves. Intelligent spirits who actually interact with the living can't be classified into simple categories. Their personalities are as varied as those of the living. Some people try to contact those who have left this world. They want to know where they are and what has happened to them. Does death hurt? Unfortunately, we never solve the mystery of what comes after death and the secrets of the universe until we have left this world. We are here to learn the lesson, but the knowledge of our time before was lost in our passage to this existence.

How did I come to write about the supernatural? Understand that this author is not a paranormal investigator or a medium and doesn't claim any psychic abilities. I am not a horror movie fan. In fact, I avoid them. I'm trained as a historian and preservationist, with a good sprinkling of curiosity thrown in. My study of the eerie experiences of Madison residents may be thought of as bizarre by those who don't believe in spooks, but researching

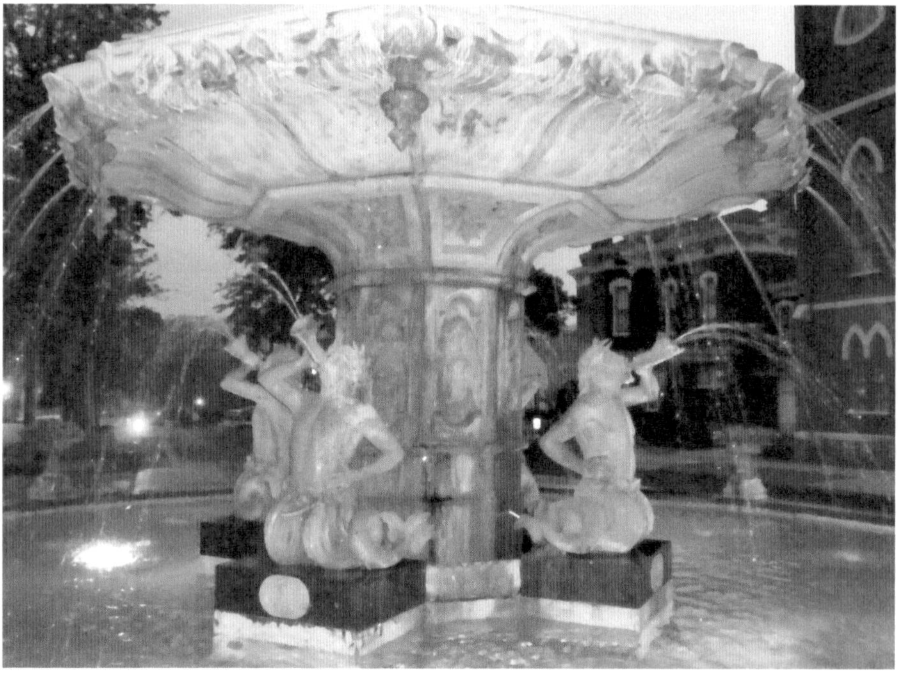

The Broadway Fountain at night.

the history of a site and trying to find out who is haunting a location is the common thread. When did they live and why did they come to stay there?

As a child growing up in Virginia, the home of my ancestors, I fell in love with the history of that state. I wanted to know everything about the old buildings we would drive past on family outings. What was inside? Who lived there? What are the stories? My mother told me about when I was five years old—we had moved from the Washington, D.C., area to Richmond, Virginia. While we were waiting for our house to be built, we lived in an apartment complex. I would knock on doors and ask the neighbors if they had any children I could play with. If they said no, I would ask if I could come inside and look around. It's funny now, and thank goodness that was a different time, but I still want to go inside and look around. Now that I know that the energy of past times may remain in the buildings, I want to know more.

Several years ago, before I decided to write about the spirits who linger and interact with this world, I had not yet experienced a tangible interaction with the other side. But since the time that I began to investigate and conduct interviews, I have had several physical encounters. This does give some credence to what some who are perceptive to the paranormal say about receptivity—that if you pay attention, you will realize that we are not alone. Many mediums even have training sessions that usually involve meditation to help you expand that ability. I don't have any desire to open that door any wider, but I now know from experience that just thinking about the other dimensions does increase your accessibility. I agree with the belief that "thought," as an energy force, creates all kinds of potential. Now I realize that thinking about, talking about or opening your mind up to psychic phenomena increases the opportunity for paranormal occurrences.

Well-known medium James Van Praagh said, "Thoughts are very subtle because they vibrate at a high frequency. Thoughts are very real, even if we can't see them. They create very real and powerful feelings and experiences."

Recently, during a holiday, I sat at a kitchen table telling my teenage grandsons Will and Byron stories about the spirits of Madison. Granddaughter Toni, who doesn't like to hear them, stayed a safe distance out of earshot of the scary tales. Meanwhile, upstairs, baby grandson Gabriel was crying and huddling in the corner of his crib, seemingly seeing something that frightened him across the room. My daughter, Lacy, came downstairs to fill a milk bottle and said, "Oh, so that's why he's staring across the room and screaming in the crib. You're down here stirring up the spirits!"

John Milton called it Purgatory, the place that we go to await judgment when we die. John Wesley believed in an intermediary state between death and the final judgment, where there is a possibility to "continue to grow in holiness." I believe that there is a place where you are given the opportunity to learn what you didn't learn while you were here on earth. But we don't all go into the same realm. Where we go is determined by the way we have lived our lives. Some mediums say that you go to the level where there are others who think like you do.

You will take what you learn in this life with you. That's why we are encouraged to be kind to others, perform civic duties, volunteer for the good, develop and take advantage of your natural gifts, expand your knowledge and live up to your potential. It is not only for the joy it gives in this life but also to develop your soul, for your eternal lessons.

Every life is as infinite as the universe. With death, our energy does change and undergo transitions and transformations. Ancient writings tell us what we need to know about the universe. They tell us of the "many other mansions of our Father" to which we will travel. I believe that these are what Einstein and other scientists recognize as dimensions. After a discussion with a physicist friend about death and other dimensions, he said, "What is in other dimensions is very small, very minute." But in death, we are not encumbered with our physical shells. We become a different form of energy, possibly small enough to fit into those dimensions.

What is it that keeps some earthbound, staying behind to haunt the living? Perhaps their lingering doesn't have anything to do with us at all. Some of them may fear what lies beyond and may feel guilt in the knowledge that they didn't live their lives as they should have. Some may wish to stay behind to protect or influence a loved one. What is it that they want us to know?

People who claim to speak to the dead tell us that they do have a message for us. We should believe in the good things that are all around us. The natural sequence for all spirits is to move up the hierarchical layers of the universe. That is done through the strength of one thing: the power of love. Regret and fear are tribulations that drag on the soul and hold it down. Release them and let go of them in this life. The love that all humans want is in your heart already, waiting for you to find it. Is this what they are trying to tell us? Most likely, the ones left behind didn't learn that lesson and are looking for the answer themselves.

Everyone makes mistakes. Some are hard to live with, but that is why we have the gift of forgiveness—not only forgiveness of others but also of ourselves. To release our anger with forgiveness is a gift. But some don't know or take advantage of this eternal gift of forgiveness, and so they are destined to suffer until they learn of its power. Some call them the damned or the lost, the ones that linger in this world, unable to move forward.

Haunted Real Estate

What is it that makes Madison so receptive to an overabundance of paranormal activity? Crystal, limestone and running water are known to be enhancers of spiritual energy. Spirits are said to need energy to exist. Madison is blessed with limestone cliffs, scores of geode stones that "grow" crystals inside and the Ohio River, with its conductive energy running along the shores. These physical factors create the perfect environs for supporting spiritual forces.

Does knowing that the spirits reside in the buildings of Madison create a hardship for sellers of the properties in town? It doesn't seem to affect sales or curb the desire of people to live in the beautiful period homes. Most of the residents consider it a privilege to live in the Landmark Historic District and become caretakers of their homes for future generations. That is part of the responsibility of living here. Maybe Madison just has an unusual number of enlightened residents who understand the nature of spiritual existence.

What if you have a property that you suspect is haunted? There are some states that require sellers to disclose hauntings that are known to have taken place at a property. Indiana has a statute in its legislation that requires disclosure of a "distressed property"—in other words, properties that have had crime, murder, death or other undesirable activities take place there. Jill Beitz, a friend who is a real estate agent in Indianapolis, said that she "stumbled into a haunted house during a showing—a big old beautiful Queen Anne. I heard knocks and footsteps while waiting for my clients. Saw a shadow person run past, too. When I asked the [listing] agent if anyone died in the house, there was a loooong pause, and he said, 'Maybe, I'm not sure.' I searched the obits and am pretty sure his own father-in-law died in the house!"

She recommended disclosure "right up front because if the neighbors know, the new buyers will find out from them the day they move in…it would just be better to not be sneaky about it and risk a lawsuit later. Most people would just laugh it off anyway or maybe even *want* a haunted house. That would at least weed out the people who may be really scared of such a thing and would possibly sue. I know some nationalities don't want to buy houses that have had bankruptcies happen in them—bad feng shui." For superstitious Hong Kongers, the building is *hongza*, a term derived from the Cantonese word *hong*, meaning violence, murder or calamity, and *za*, meaning residence.

New Jersey requires reporting of "a property purportedly being haunted." In North Carolina, an agent or seller must answer if asked, but if the buyer does not ask, then they are not required to say that the property has had activity. And even then, they don't have to tell exactly what has happened, only that there has been a report of paranormal activity, which could mean any level of action. California and Hawaii both require by law that sellers report any supernatural events that have occurred at a property. Given the presence of the regulations, paranormal activity is clearly recognized by the legal systems of many states as having taken place.

Whitehall Bed-and-Breakfast

Millions of spiritual creatures walk the earth Unseen, both when we wake, and when we sleep.
—John Milton, Paradise Lost

1251 West Main Street

At first morning light, the young couple in their mid-twenties, looking rumpled and groggy, headed toward the large wood-paneled door. They had an opportunity to quickly tell the proprietors of the bed-and-breakfast what prompted their hasty exit, but only because the Murphys had come to the foyer to greet them after their stay the night before in the Green Room suite.

Sometime during the night, both had awakened from a cozy slumber under the lace-trimmed bed coverings of the canopied bed to find an elderly lady sitting in the chair next to them. As she sat by the river-view window, she didn't seem to be as upset by their presence as much as they were by hers. She was dressed in the style worn during the 1860s, when the site was the home of the Union surgeon who oversaw the large Civil War hospital located west of the house. The couple felt a sense of fear wash over them. Realizing that they both saw the vision, and that she was not of this world, they cautiously slipped out of the room to the chamber in between the two bedrooms and out the balcony door. It was a long, uncomfortable night because the wicker love seat and chair on the balcony were not intended for peaceful sleeping. Morning didn't come soon enough, but when it did, the two packed their bags and high-tailed it down the stairs and toward the door. After a swift explanation, they were out the door and on their way. Well, they did take a great story away with them, one that I am certain was retold for years to come.

The suites at Whitehall Bed-and-Breakfast are stunning, with world-class antiques purchased in the lower South and brought to the high-ceiling rooms. Richly detailed Victorian furniture is used throughout. Tall poster beds, with canopies or half-testers, are found in every bedroom, dressed with thick, luxurious bed coverings. Every corner holds a feast for the eyes in the form of beautiful objects. A sumptuous breakfast, served in the formal dining room at precisely 9:00 a.m., comes with your stay. The first mouthwatering course, of puréed fresh fruit and aromatic fresh baked muffins, is followed by not one but two entrées. That morning, the filet mignon and chicken l'orange that Mr. Murphy had specially cut for him by the local butcher were cooked to perfection. And if you can force another delicious bite in, dessert of cheesecake or key lime pie is placed before you. Betty Murphy prepares the delicacies, placed artfully on antique china, while Bill Murphy serves

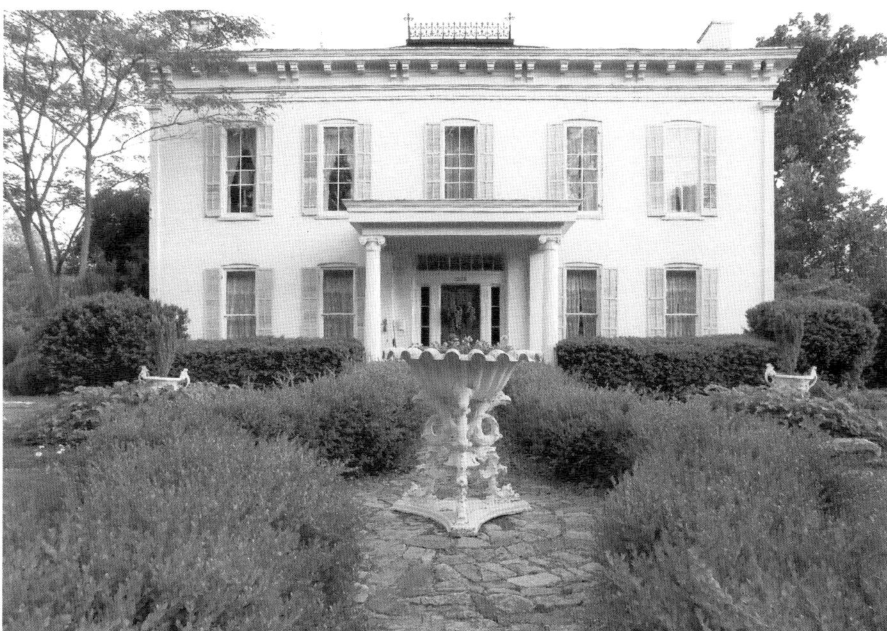

Beautiful Whitehall Bed-and-Breakfast, at the farthest west end of Madison. The rooms have wonderful Ohio River views. The spirits love them.

with panache and retells local tales. Both of the Murphys are retired teachers from Battle Creek, Michigan, who made their longtime dream come true.

The house was built in 1827–28, likely by Judge David B. Cummins, but sadly he passed away soon after its completion. His widow sold the house, and by 1844, it was being auctioned off on the steps of the courthouse.

During the Civil War, one of the Union's largest military hospitals sat directly to the west of the house. The thirty-seven-acre complex of the Madison General Hospital was opened in 1863. Surgeon General Gabriel Grant, the director of the hospital, lived in the home. Some say that surgeries took place inside the house, but it seems unlikely when so many other buildings were available for those procedures. But in any case, we know of the immense suffering that occurred in these hospitals and of the energy left behind from those emotions and sudden deaths. After the war, a town sprang up in the old buildings, lived in mostly by laborers employed in occupations associated with the river trades. Later, the buildings were disassembled or moved intact to various streets throughout town. You can see many of the shotguns along West Main Street that are believed to have been part of the hospital compound. Madison had sent more troops to the war effort than any other town in Indiana and also suffered the greatest number of soldiers lost.

In 1890, the house became the West Madison Public School, the name lasting for the next twenty-five years. Initials of the children still remain on the walls. Many children moved through the building, bringing their boundless energy to the area. That may explain the sound of children's laughter heard at various times running up and down the stairs and through the hallways when no children are in the house.

During the 1930s, the Great Depression also brought about dismal changes here. The house was partitioned off into apartments in 1937 and soon slid into a sequence of renters. In spite of its glorious beginnings, by the time the Murphys purchased the property in 1991, it had nearly fallen into a state of collapse. But they had a goal, and they brought their vision, enthusiasm and stamina to work through the restoration of the home.

Bill was working on and living in the building by himself, while because of the primitive conditions, Betty remained at their former home in Michigan. In order to get to the second floor, he had to climb a ladder while the stairs were being reconstructed. It wasn't long after he began working on the building when, one evening, while wrapped in his sleeping bag up on the second floor and in the middle of a deep sleep, Bill awoke to horrendous crashing and banging on the floors below. Thinking that vandals had broken in and were doing terrible damage, he rushed down to the main floor, shovel in hand, ready to defend his property. But when he got to the location of all the noises, no one was there and nothing was out of place. At first, he thought that maybe he was just dreaming. But with subsequent nights of spectral crashes and shattering, he began to understand that he was not there alone.

When his son, Ben, joined him in his restoration efforts, the evening commotions did not stop. When construction had progressed enough for Betty to move into the building site, the pair tried to explain the unexplainable to wife and mother so that she wouldn't be as shocked as they had been. At first, she was skeptical, but the ongoing nightly performances convinced her otherwise. Many spirits object quite vigorously when the buildings they inhabit are changed through construction. It's one of the most frequently reported triggers for paranormal activity. Because they've become accustomed to the area in which they have taken up residence, they let observers know that they are not happy by displaying tumultuous temper tantrums. Maybe old Judge Cummins thought that someone was modifying his original house plans. The nighttime ruckus continued with regularity until the project was completed.

The nightly crashes ceased, but they found that the poltergeist now began to manifest itself in several different forms, and there seemed to be more than one entity inhabiting their home. The Murphys hired a dear older lady named Ella to help clean the rooms on occasion. In one of the suites, she would mention that there were cold spots and that someone was calling her name. Bill said that Ella had a different way of saying, "Yes." She would say, "Ahhyeaayes!" quite loudly. He said that when she was working, he could hear her in the other room talking. He asked her who she was talking to. She said that she heard someone calling her name in the suites, and she would reply, "Ahhyeaayes!" Betty hears her name called, too. So do some of the visitors, during the daytime and the night.

I had a wonderful stay at the bed-and-breakfast, before moving to Madison. My husband and I would visit Madison every year from our home in nearby Columbus, Indiana. I had told him that we would move there one day and soaked in every detail of our visits to the beautiful historic city. I tried many times to reserve our stay at the Whitehall Bed-and-Breakfast, but to my disappointment, it was always booked. Finally, I called for reservations early enough in the year to snag a suite at the inn. When we arrived, I happily admired the beauty of the Green Room suite, named for the brilliant color of its walls.

On the first of our two-night stay, I was getting ready to go to bed and had turned off all the lights. Only the moonlight coming through the windows lit my way to the bed. When passing by the sitting room, I very clearly began to hear what sounded like booted footsteps on the wooden floors. They sounded loud and heavy. There was no mistaking exactly where that sound was coming from. Knowing that no living person was in that room, I ran like a frightened child and leaped into the bed, pulling the covers over my head. It took a little longer than usual to fall asleep that night, as I waited and listened for noises in the next room. I didn't hear them again and drifted off to sleep sometime in the night. The next morning, I cautiously looked where I had heard the footsteps coming from and was shocked to see carpeted flooring!

At breakfast, I asked the owners if there were ever any reports of unusual happenings. They asked what kind of "happenings." I told them the story of the footsteps, and Mr. Murphy said, "Oh, that's nothing. That happens all the time." Another couple, also staying at the B&B, stared, listening with silent interest. They said that they were both employed in law enforcement in Indianapolis. I wondered if they were believers or if they thought we were "a little off." Bill asked if my makeup had been moved around. I said no. He explained that in my rooms, a female ghost likes to move around the lady's makeup. She doesn't have anything to do with the men's items. Sometimes the smell of heavy perfume is detected in the rooms. One couple, a contractor and his wife from New Hampshire, reported that her makeup had been moved around from where she had placed it, as have others. That evening, I took note of where my toiletries were placed as I prepared for bed. I made my husband wait until I was under the covers before turning the lights out.

The Helpful Nurse

Owner Betty Murphy later told me that she awoke one evening to find a woman standing over her by the bed. The apparition was transparent, as Betty noted that she could see the rest of the room right through her. She remained there, looking at Betty for a moment before she started to disappear from her feet, going up to her head, until she was gone.

Another guest, Marilyn Tanner, who is a frequent visitor at Whitehall, has repeatedly felt the presence of a female spirit who seemed "helpful."

One evening, while sleeping in one of the immense suites, she awoke with a chill and began to reach down to pull up the blankets at her feet. Before she could reach them, they raised and came up to cover her. She then saw the older lady specter standing by her bed. From what Marilyn could tell, there in the dark that night, she seemed to have a look of concerned interest on her tired, kindly face. I believe that she was one of the nurses who worked long, weary hours at the busy hospital during the Civil War, still lingering in the old house and taking care of her charges. The great emotional toll that the war took on many souls would explain the remaining energy still reverberating in the house.

Marilyn explained to the spirit, "You are not alive anymore. Look at the light and go into it. You have done your duty for long enough." She told the Murphys about her experience and what she had done. Betty thinks that the benevolent spirit took her advice, as the Murphys have not heard any more reports about her from their guests. Sometimes poltergeist lay low for months or years, only to return when some action provokes a response, created by just the right conditions. Maybe she has gone on to find the peace that she deserves. Maybe.

THE CENTRAL STREET LADY IN WHITE

Know then, unnumber'd Spirits round thee fly,
The light Militia of the lower sky.
—Alexander Pope

317 Central Street

A friend in Madison told me the story of when he lived in this house with his former wife.

The new owners were recently married and had purchased the home on Central Street as their first, together. They both had a love of old buildings. Mike is an outgoing architect with steel-gray eyes that look straight at you when he talks to you. He freely shares his knowledge of local history. His wife, Brigette, is a friendly, attractive blonde and a talented microbiologist.

They enjoyed taking part in Civil War reenactments and would travel to and camp at various historic sites. That is actually how the couple met, with Brigette attending a reenactment in which Mike was taking part. It was one of those electric moments when they first saw each other. Brigette found that she loved participating in the reenactments, too. Soon she was wearing a nineteenth century–style wedding dress. Their wedding took place at one of the reenactments, with period-dressed attendees and the celebration cannons firing in their honor.

The house that they chose to start their married life in is a gray, two-story brick Federal row house that was built in 1848. It has a rare arched

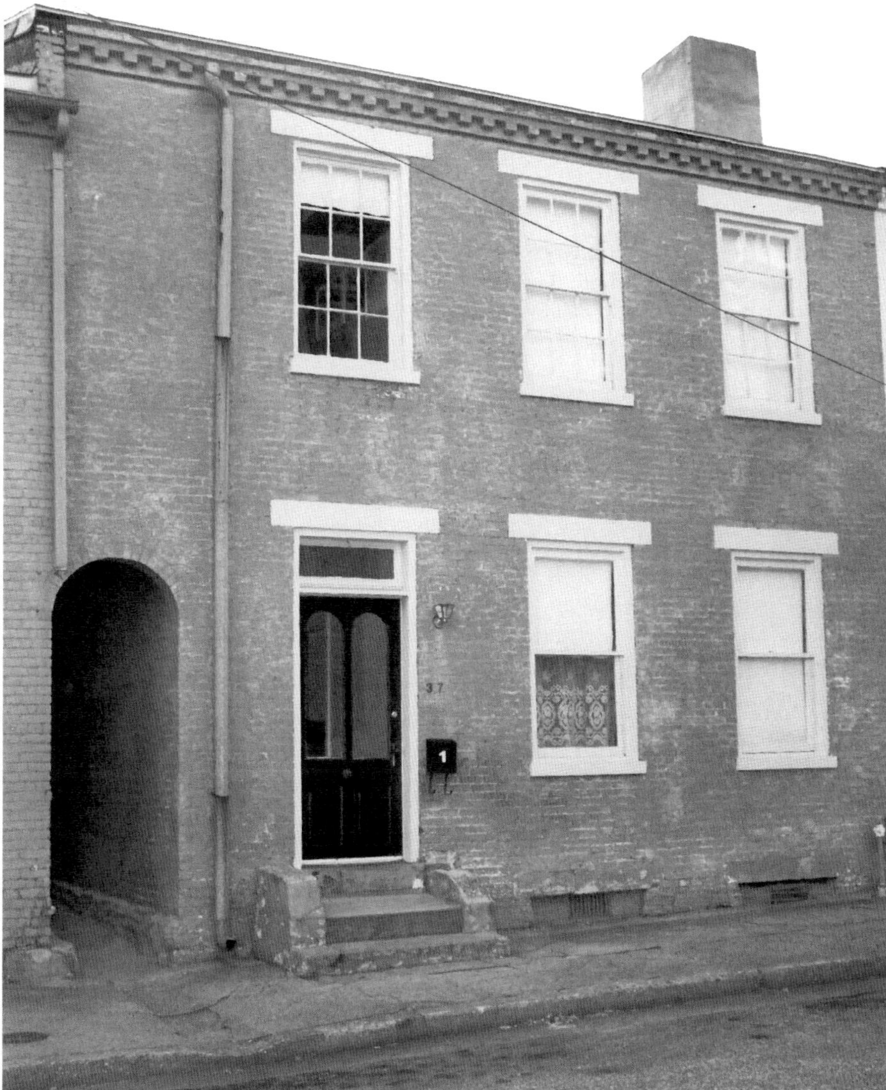

The Central Street home of the Lady in White.

walkthrough to their back courtyard, and the house sits in the middle of town on a street that runs south off Main Street. In more recent years, it was converted into two apartments, one on each floor. The couple purchased the house with the intention of restoring it to its former glory as a single-family dwelling. But there was an obstacle to fulfilling that goal: the two male tenants who occupied the upstairs would not leave.

The tenants were of questionable character and had curious activities involving the strange smells of burning herbs. They came and went in and out of the house but never spoke to Mike or Brigette. They had been told that the pending sale would require them to move. But they were still there when Mike and Brigette moved in. Apparently, they did not feel any immediate necessity to locate a new residence.

Mike and Brigitte began to paint and make repairs to the main floor. They loved their new home, even with the tension caused by the presence of the unwanted upstairs occupants. One evening, Mike was standing in the hallway and saw Brigette move to the back of the kitchen and through the doorway to the left, leading into the porch. Mike followed her, but when he got to the porch, Brigette was not there. A moment later, she came out of the pantry at the opposite side of the room. She had been in there for a while. It took a few minutes for Mike to comprehend that he had just experienced his first encounter with the Lady in White. She was similar in build to Brigette, of medium height, with flowing blond hair and dressed in a late nineteenth century–style white dress. She had seemed to move smoothly through the room, without the need to take steps, as if floating. "Women in white" are reported to be seen in haunted environments all over the world. It's thought that they represent sadness or loss or are said to be searching for something.

One night, Brigette was sitting in her bed, wrapped in multicolored quilts. It was dark in the house except for the glow of the television she was watching. Suddenly, she felt a cold breeze move by her as if someone had opened a door on a cold winter night. But no one had opened a door, or a window for that matter. She was alone in the house. She looked around, seeking an explanation. There was no one there, but she knew what it was as the hairs stood up on the back of her neck. The Lady in White was just making her rounds through the house, announced by the telling breeze and temperature drop.

On another occasion, Brigette was washing the dishes at the sink when she felt a presence move behind her and then a finger poking at her back. Thinking that it was Mike giving her a love tap, she turned around to find that no one was there.

Mike has had experiences with spirits in other buildings in town, told in another chapter. Many will hear spirits or feel them, but he has a proclivity to seeing apparitions. I believe that his ability comes from his openness to their existence and his closeness to nature. He said, "We all see them; some of us just realize what we are seeing." I think that Brigette's closeness to Mike has now opened her to that realm, too.

Mike thought about the recent phantom sightings and decided to do a little investigative work. First, he got on the phone and called the former owner. He asked him if there had been any past reports of unusual activities in the house. "No, not that I've heard," came the reply.

About ten minutes after hanging up, the man called back and told Mike to call the man from whom he had bought the house. So Mike called him and asked the same question. The man paused for a minute and recalled that some of his tenants had mentioned strange things happening in the house. Mike asked how many of the former tenants had reported those encounters. The man thought for a minute and said, "Six out of ten." Mike had a feeling he knew what the man would answer, but he went ahead and asked him, "What kind of strange things did they report?" "Well," the man began, "they would hear footsteps upstairs when there was no one there. And they would set things down in the house and find that they had been moved around. " When Mike hung up the phone, he was armed with the knowledge of what he had suspected all along, reinforcing his conclusions. There was at least one other resident, though of a spiritual nature, in the house. By then, many people would be packing and calling the realtors, but Mike really didn't seem to mind sharing his living space with someone or something from another time.

After several weeks with no indication from the tenants upstairs that they planned on moving out, Mike decided to enlist the aid of the seemingly benevolent, if otherworldly, resident. Now, some may think it is odd to talk to a spirit, much less ask for help from one. But Mike was at the end of his patience, so he decided that it couldn't hurt. He spoke to her, saying, "Now, you know that we have the best intentions for the home. We want to put it back the way it used to be, as a family home. If you could do something to get rid of the ones upstairs, we could get that done." Not knowing if his request would do any good at all, he went back to his work on the restoration of the house.

Within two days, the keys were swinging from the apartment door. The upper floor was empty. The drawers in the dressers had been left open. The tenants had left quickly—very quickly. They never said a word to Mike or to Brigette when they left. They never even came back for their deposit.

Mike and Brigette say that it has been very quiet since their former tenants left. They have not seen or felt the Lady in White since then either. Their restoration has been completed, and the home is now a one-family residence. The Lady in White seems to be content with it that way.

SPIRIT NOTES

Every man takes the limits of his own field of vision for the limits of the world.
—Arthur Schopenhauer

Most of us wonder what happens after death. Our upbringing during childhood has some influence over what we believe. But we also have the opportunity to learn of possibilities other than what we have been taught in our youth. Those who have had near-death encounters tell of similar experiences during those moments. They recall rising above their bodies, going through a tunnel of light and being met by people they know. This is the same process that mediums say spirits recount to them as having occurred at the time of their death. But where do we really go? I guess we will have to wait and see to be certain.

In the early nineteenth century, because of social pressures, people were not allowed to acknowledge in public the presence of spirits. If one encountered unexplainable events, they were forced to tell themselves that it was their imaginations. People who spoke of seeing spirits were thought of as being "affected," or insane, and could ultimately be committed to the asylum. To this day, you may meet people who think that interacting with the spirit world is akin to devil worship, a view lingering from that belief system.

It was only after the American Civil War that the stories of lost souls began to be told out in the open. The horrible deaths that took place with such speed necessitated equally swift burial, often without identifying the

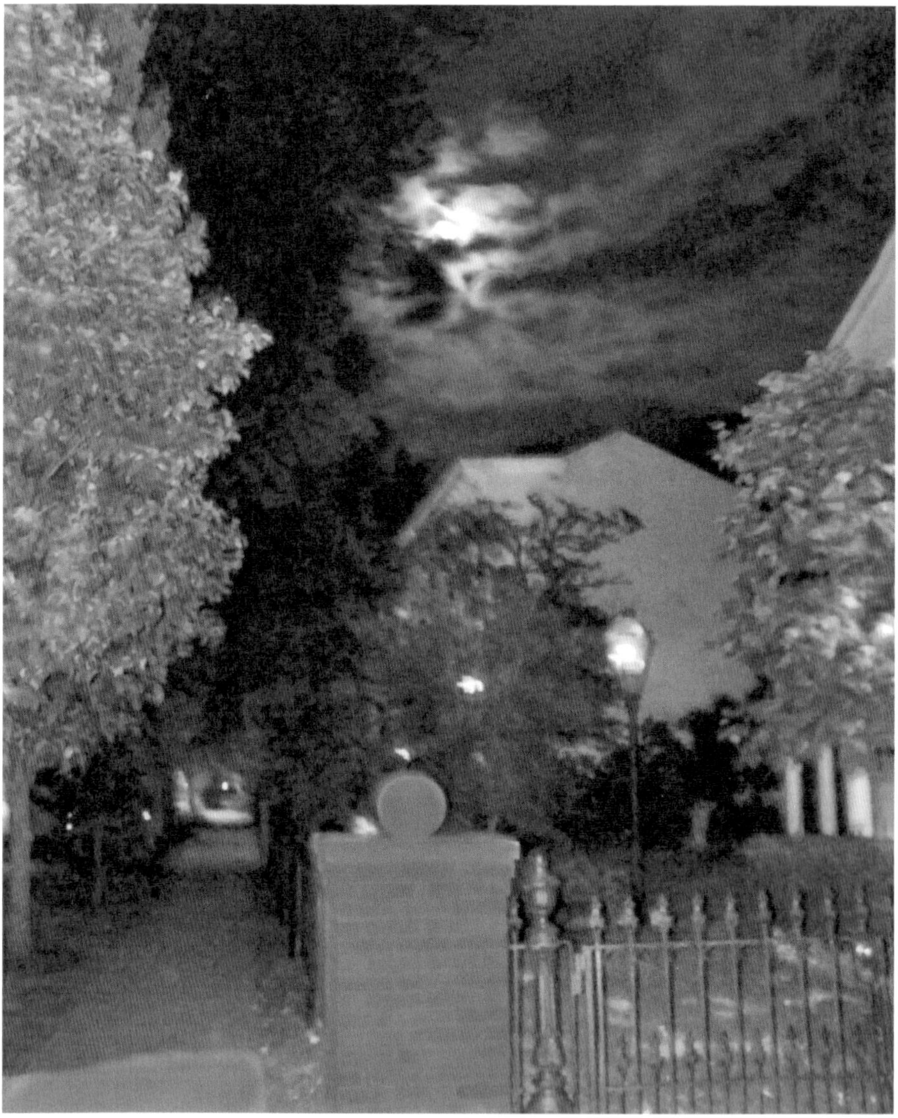

Moonlight over Madison, 300 block of West Third Street.

deceased. Not knowing where their loved ones were inspired the telling of tales of spirits wandering their way home, either not realizing that they were deceased or looking for their "right and proper" resting spot in the family burial plot.

There was an episode of the old TV show *The Twilight Zone* in which line after line of Civil War soldiers were seen walking down a road past an old plantation. The young lady of the plantation addressed many of the soldiers, inquiring if they had seen her husband. One of the soldiers found peace for a night on the veranda of her home only to discover the next day that he, along with all the other soldiers, is making the final journey home—as was the young lady, who had been shot days before by a stray bullet as she rocked on her front porch.

Spirits have always existed. Some religions tell us that we all existed as spirits before receiving an earthly body and that we will again after our time here has finished but before we once again are given a body. The spirits who did not choose to receive earthly bodies are known as demons. They usually appear to do the bidding of their master, the "great deceiver," and to create malice. Interaction with this type of entity is best left to professional demonologists, who are better equipped to handle these dangerous beings. That's why using a Ouija board is discouraged; you don't know what may come through the portal that may be opened.

There are different types of haunting. Most people place them in three main categories. The first is the one just discussed, the demon. The second and most common type of haunting is by spirits who are able to interact with us and try to make us aware of their existence. This type of entity is an intelligent life force that can use energy to make its presence known. This can be accomplished via many methods in their arsenal, such as chilling or warming the air; appearing as a smoky shape, in a transparent human form, as an orb or as a dark shadow; making loud, banging noises, startling family pets; or by pranks such as moving objects around or hiding them and then replacing them. I hate it when they do that. You know you just had it. Then you find it right in front of you. Yes, they are just playing with you.

These hauntings are thought to be by spirits who, when they died, did not move on to where they were suppose to go. They are known as earthbound spirits. Many reasons have been given as to why these spirits do not move on to where they are supposed to go after death. Unfinished business is always mentioned with these spirits. Avenging or solving their own untimely deaths is another. Or they may have missed their time to "go to the light." They may also be "attached" to a person, building or object and are sticking around to protect it.

Not realizing that they are dead is another theory, but some professionals debate whether spirits do or do not know of their deaths. Some of these professionals say that the spirit can see their body when they rise above it and definitely know they are dead. But other experts have come into contact with spirits who seem oblivious to their own deaths. For whatever reason, they are "here" and will interact with the human or animal whose attention they can reach.

The last main form of paranormal activity is residual action. This is an energy that repeats itself, replaying the same motion. How this occurs is interesting to think about. Is it a rip in time that we accidently look into and view? How does this energy exist in a manner that we can actually see it from another time? This type of activity is often triggered by weather conditions, or it may occur on the same date or time every day, month or year.

All of these types of haunting are found in Madison. People who live here just shrug and nod, as if to say, "What can you tell me that I don't already know?" In Madison, even the most skeptical soon understand that we share our space with ghosts. It's just a matter of when they come to that conclusion, not if.

Because those who talk to the spirits say that they are around us at all times, I believe that old houses come with spirits who are just as surprised to see us as we are to see them. Some of us know that the veil between this world and the next is thin. That tells me that they are here but not in what some refer to as the same dimension. Psychics tell us that spirits of our relatives and ancestors are often with us. That concept is also a common belief of many cultures. But the spirits who don't know us seem to be the ones that give us the most trouble, unless one of your late relatives has an unresolved problem with you.

After interviewing so many residents who live in the houses and experience the paranormal activity, I find that there is a common thread among nearly all of these plucky characters. It was very surprising to me that the majority report that they are unafraid; they are just startled at the knowledge that they are living with something from beyond this world—an attitude surprisingly free of the usual Hollywood horror-filled reactions expected at such a discovery.

THE HAUNTED FUNERAL PARLOR

How many of our daydreams would darken into nightmares, were there a danger of their coming true!
—Logan Pearsall Smith

402 West Main Street

This rambling red brick Queen Anne–style building is situated on West Main Street on one of the most visible corners in town. Madison is a favorite weekend destination, and many tourists take the carriage rides offered at several locations on Main Street. The paired horses pull carriages by the building in the evening, and many walkers move past the site without realizing the tragic circumstances that took place inside.

Funeral homes see their share of the sadness that accompanies the loss of loved ones. They try to do their best for the families by treating their passed loved ones with respect. But we know that by the time the bodies get to the funeral home, they are only empty shells in which earthly lives were once contained. By then, the spirit has gone on to its just reward—at least, in most cases.

From the early times to the recent past, people have been born and have died at home. So nearly every home in town has experienced the death of someone who, after preparations, was then laid out in the parlor. Announcements were placed in the local newspaper, inviting the public in to "view the remains." This is where the name "funeral parlor" came from.

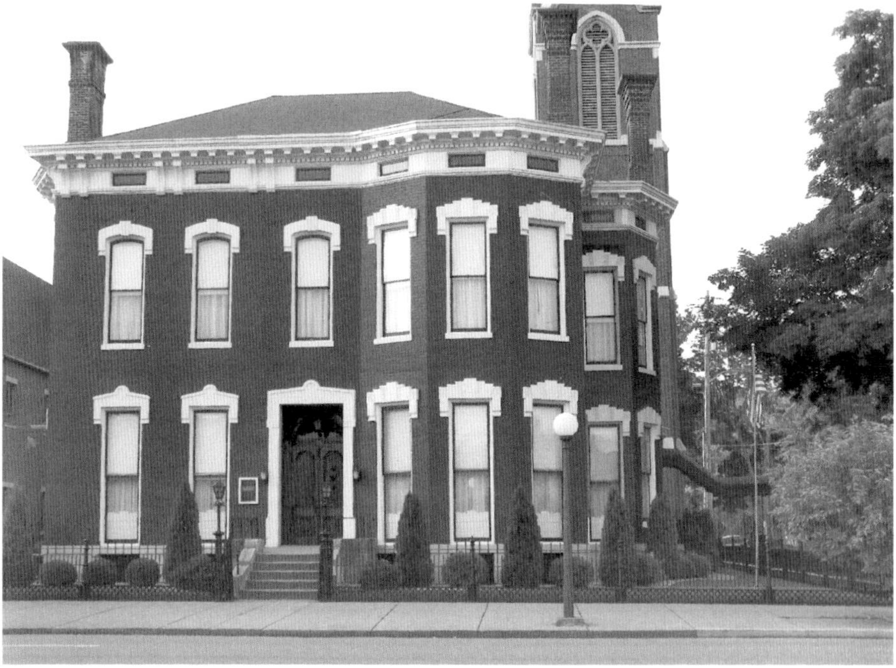

402 West Main Street, former home of the Vail-Holt Funeral Home.

What was to become the Hail-Volt Funeral Home was started in 1839 by Cornelius Vail and J.W. White at 109–111 West Main Street. They made furniture and burial caskets hewn with hardwoods gathered from the thick nearby forests. They also arranged burials. It's been said that they were involved in the funerals of President Zachary Taylor and Vice President John C. Calhoun. Cornelius was a craftsman who inherited his considerable talents from his master shipbuilding father, who built ships during the War of 1812. It became a family business when he bought out Mr. White and formed a partnership with his own son. The business was moved in 1924 to the 402 West Main Street site.

In 1937, the business owned a twenty-foot hearse with a 120 horsepower engine, advertised as "luxurious enough for kings and queens." The location on Main Street now offered on-site funeral services. By 1959, the company could boast of having recorded more than twenty-five thousand burials. In 1973, Cornelius's great-grandson, Dana Vale, formed a partnership with John Holt. Dana passed away within a year of their partnership. Businesses

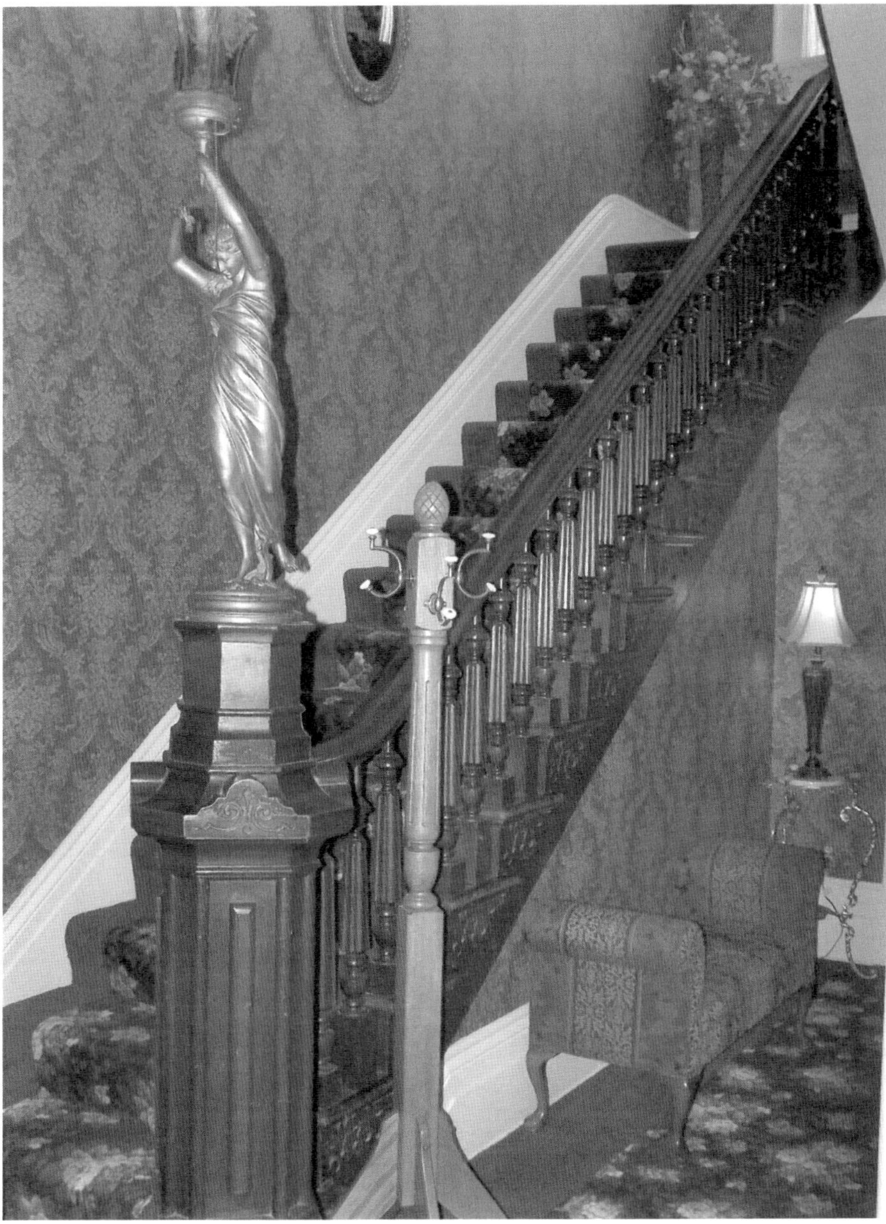

Staircase where a grief-stricken matron committed suicide and refused to cross over.

evolve in order to survive, and this one became part of a large nationwide conglomerate but still operated two area locations.

Madison has attracted many men who accumulated huge amounts of wealth. The building at 402 West Main Street had long been the private home of wealthy residents. It was built by well-known citizen Captain Nathan Powell. Captain Powell was reported to travel in elite circles and yet was kind and generous to the less fortunate. At the time of his death, in July 1882, his estate was valued at $1.2 million.

By 1911, the house, then known as the "Sage Property," was purchased from Joseph Craven by Oliver W.H. Roe, who was a resident of North Madison. His mother was coming to Madison from Petoskey, Michigan, to live with her son at the property. She had been widowed twice, first from Dr. John L. Roe and then from the late Judge Friedley, and was "reported to have suffered for some time with an attack of light paralysis."

When Mr. Roe, the son, died, he left his mother possession of the property. Her sorrow at his death transformed her mind, distorted it and swallowed her sanity. Finally, one evening, she lost all grasp on reality. She ordered that her staff gather at the stair bottom to hear an announcement. As she descended the stairs, she paused as though she was about to speak to them. With a quick movement, she pulled out a gun, put it to her head and fired. The horrified staff retained that image as the last memory of their former mistress.

The house was purchased and sold several times with quick procession after the "incident" until it was purchased in 1924 as the site of preparation for last remembrances. Employees spoke of seeing shadows and hearing voices around the staircase. They set objects down in one place only to find them later in a different room completely. One former employee was working in the basement late at night and said that he felt like someone was watching him for sometime; he was scared out of his wits by the unmistakable feeling of someone tapping him on the shoulder. Economic circumstances brought about the consolidation of services, and the building was offered for sale in the fall of 2011.

Some will not enter the site. They don't want to be in the same place with the former owner who lost her mind but never left the building. Some who come there don't know the history of the location but just have an eerie feeling. Many former employees report having seen her appear and heard her on the stairs. They tell of hearing whispers in the hallway. One thing is certain: the new owners won't be alone in the house.

The Old Lumber Mill

Do we not hear voices, gentle and great, and some of them like the voices of departed friends, do we not hear them saying to us, "Come up hither?"
—William Mountford

721 West First Street

The Old Lumber Mill was built on the Corner of Plum and First Streets in 1854. It had been built as one of several mills known as the Star Mills, owned by W.W. Page. It was operated as a mill on and off for more than one hundred years.

Today, it is a popular antique mall, full of choice items on all three floors. I brought my antiques business with me when I moved to Madison. I have sold antiques in several antique malls throughout central and southern Indiana, but some have felt more "right" than others. The feeling at the Lumber Mill Antique Mall was right for me. I love the thrill of the hunt for "treasures." And just because I sell in a certain location doesn't mean that I can't shop there, too. In fact, it usually means that I *will* be shopping there. I think that dealers are one another's best customers.

A few months after moving my business, I was up on the top floor, where consignment furniture sits in the large open room, with massive exposed ceiling beams (from the time when the building was a working lumber mill). I was alone and began to feel uneasy, like there was someone following me around. I don't like that feeling, so I hurried down the stairs to where there

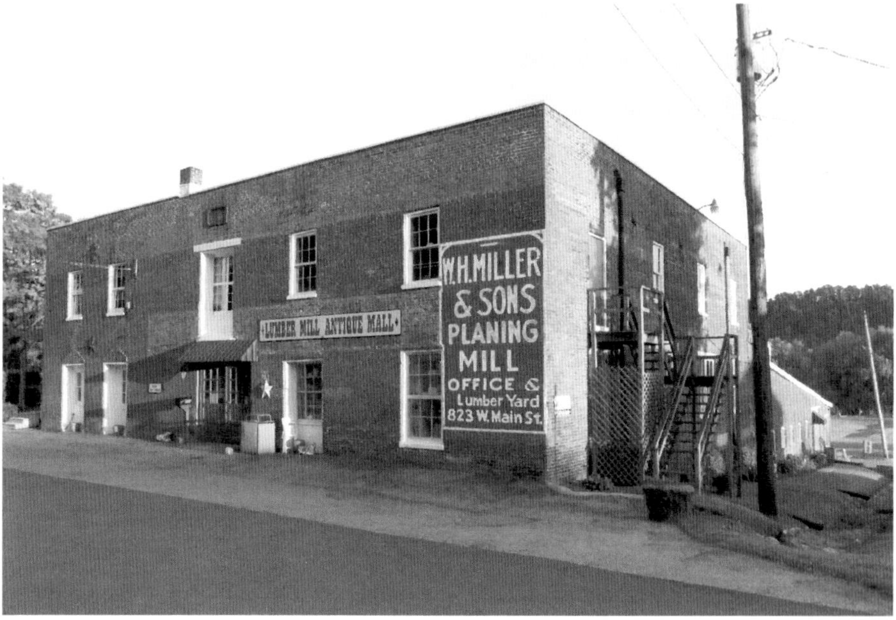

Today, the Lumber Mill Antique Mall hosts many spirits. Some are attached to the many antiques for sale in the building, and others are from the building's past.

were other people shopping. I asked a former employee if she knew of any unusual occurrences in the antique mall over the years. She said that sometimes they can hear furniture moving around on the top floor when there is no one up there. And when they go to investigate, nothing is out of place.

Some say that spirits can become "attached" to locations. There have also been cases of spirits attaching to items to see what happens to them. Now, I really am very fond of some of my finds and of some of my heirlooms, but I don't think I want to stick around in the afterlife to hold on to any of them. But I am fond enough of antiques in this life to take the risk of running into possessive spirits by going up on the third floor to shop, even though I still get goose bumps and that strange feeling. I just don't stay up there for very long.

THE CURIOUS SPIRIT

Pity is for the living, envy is for the dead.
—Mark Twain

511 Broadway

The house looked huge. It was one of the beautiful brick row house styles that I had always admired. I was able to get in touch with the owners by calling the phone number on their "For Sale by Owner" sign displayed in the front window. A woman's friendly voice answered and said they were on their way to the house at that very time and that she would be glad to show me the house. They had used it as a vacation home for themselves, family and friends. Madison is like that. Many people want to move here when they are caught by the charm of the town. Some purchase a home as soon as possible. Some make plans to move here when they retire. Others purchase a vacation home where they can spend their leisure time.

The current owners—Dick, a retired dentist, and Dorothy, his outgoing wife—were going to meet me and my husband to show us the interior. It was very elegant, and they had made a lot of repairs and upgrades in the twenty-one years that they had owned the house. We were thinking that this might be the one for us. I asked for permission to take some pictures so that I could see how furniture arrangements would work. They granted it, so I snapped away throughout our tour. I really liked the house, but we had not

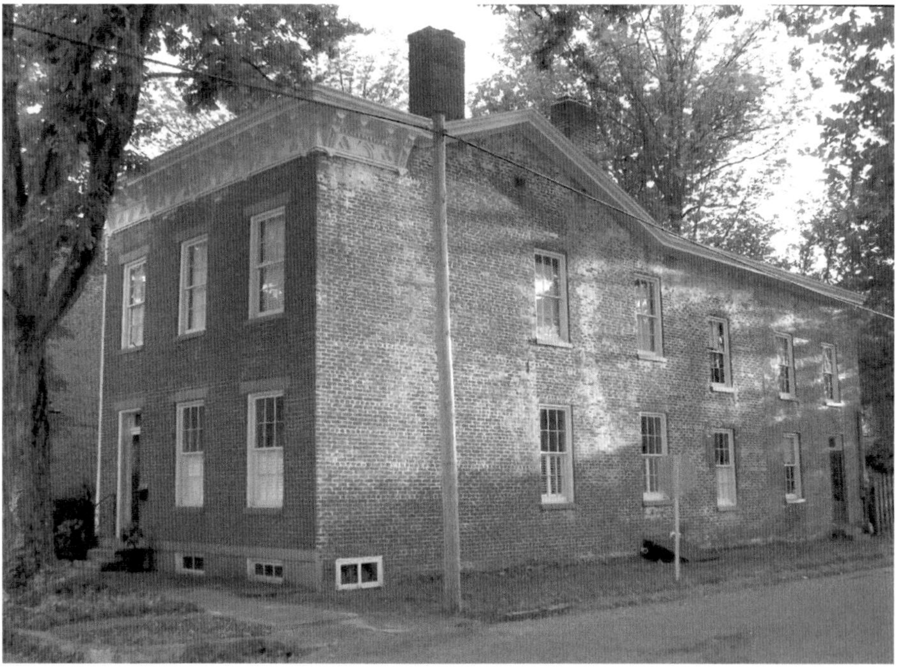

This photo of the house was taken during a time when my husband and I were interested in its purchase. At one time, there was a bakery in the rear of the building. Many houses had businesses that operated out of the owner's home.

looked at any other homes and I decided to look at one around the corner. We did end up purchasing that home around the corner because it more closely fit our needs.

I didn't think much about the pictures that I had taken in the house on Broadway until later. When I looked at the pictures, I saw a "figure" that I can only describe as a presence. I had taken about a dozen photos, and this presence was in two of them. I knew what I was looking at. I have never seen anything like this show up in one of my photos, before or since then. Had I captured a curious and maybe lonely spirit following us around? After all, as a vacation home, the house stood vacant most of the time. Maybe he was just unhappy that his space was being invaded, as spirits often are. Or perhaps he was simply checking out the new visitors.

Two years later, I came to know and work on several projects with a former owner of the property, Link Ludington. I asked him if he recalled any odd occurrences in the house. He said, "No, but a man died in the house." Research on the house found that the first owner was a merchant

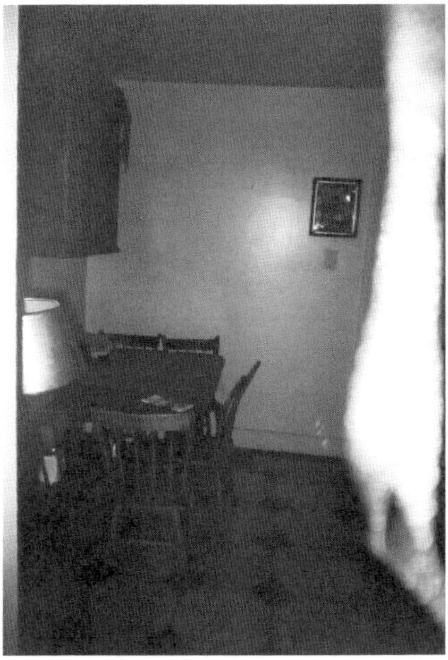

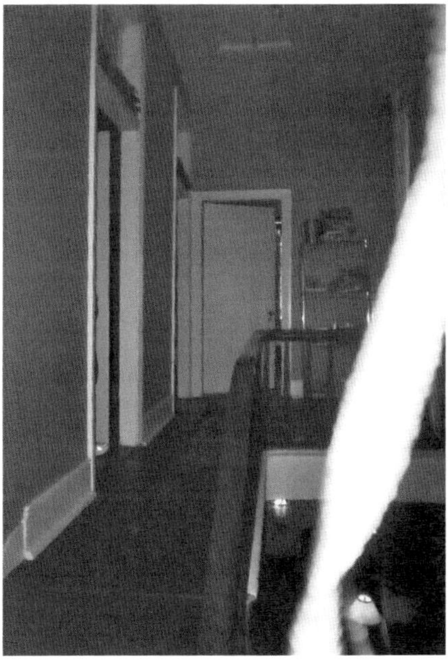

named Alfred Dunning, who had built the house in 1849. In the 1859–60 Madison City Business Directory, he is listed as a grocer. His younger brother, twenty-six-year-old Duncan Dunbar Dunning, had come to visit him in December 1852 and, a few days later, had died in the house. The *Madison Republican* reported that on January 3, 1853, the International Order of Odd Fellows "turned out" to honor Duncan Dunning. The Odd Fellows had an impressive impact on the city of Madison in many ways.

The mission of the Odd Fellows organization was to "visit the sick, relieve the distressed, bury the dead and educate the orphan." It was responsible for bringing the Broadway Fountain from the World's Fair of 1876 and giving it to the city of Madison in 1882. The fountain is one of the best-known landmarks in Madison. Young couples hold their weddings there and have engagement photos taken there. The oldest farmer's market in the state of Indiana sets up in the summer

Top: I didn't really think about the anomalies in the photos we took at first. Many months later, I took out the photos and realized what I was looking at. As we were reviewing the premises, we were being observed by someone or something. This was in the kitchen of the house.

Bottom: A poltergeist is following us around on our tour of the house. The entity flowing up the stairs shows a manifestation that is clearly with us as we toured the home. I suppose that it was sizing us up as we were considering the purchase of the property.

there, and monthly concerts are held at the fountain as well. Although the organization was originally looking for a drinking fountain, it was offered such a good deal on this fountain that it purchased it. It was originally cast in iron, but one hundred years later, it was so deteriorated that the residents of the city raised the funds to recast it in bronze. The fountain is located one block south of 511 Broadway. Could the spirit of Duncan Dunbar Dunning be the specter who had curiously followed us around the house that day? Is he still there, spending eternity in the house where his young life ended?

If not Duncan, who? There are other possibilities. There had also been a small family cemetery located across the street from the house. A building was built on the property to house elderly women who were unable to care for themselves—that today still stands as medical offices. No records exist, and to anyone's knowledge it was never moved, so to this day the bodies may still remain under the building. That would not be as unusual as one might think. Many family cemeteries were forgotten and lost after one generation. Many times, spirits are unhappy with the treatment of their grave sites. Perhaps this one saw some activity in the old neighbor house and decided to come over and investigate.

DONLAN HOUSE

HAUNTED HARMONIES

Aërial spirits, by great Jove design'd
To be on earth the guardians of mankind:
Invisible to mortal eyes they go,
And mark our actions, good or bad, below:
The immortal spies with watchful care preside,
And thrice ten thousand round their charges glide
They can reward with glory or with gold,
A power they by Divine permission hold.
—Hesiod

102 West Third Street

When I talked that day with the friendly volunteer Laurle Clemens, she was busy working at the Jefferson County Historical Society. She and husband Ben live in a rambling Queen Anne/Romanesque red brick home with a three-story turret on the eastern side of the house and lots of carved decorative wooden trim covering a round front porch. Like so many in town, an ornate iron fence surrounds the property, likely installed to protect the yard from escapees at a time when hogs were run down the streets to market. Built in about 1895, the house sits on a highly traveled corner, at West Third and West Street, one block north of Main Street. It is a striking building and draws so much interest that people stop by to take photographs and admire the highly detailed elements of the house. A brick mason once stopped by to discuss the fine brick patterns used on the house. A couple from England who were visiting Madison struck up a conversation with Laurle about her yard decorations.

Laurle and Ben love World War II–era music so much that they have speakers wired throughout the home, that play the music, both inside and out. As you pass by the house, the music plays for all within earshot to enjoy. Often, after having gone out, they would return home to find their music playing, even though they knew that they had turned it off before they left. It switched on during the day and night by itself. They have had the wiring checked out several times. It is all in fine working order. The very first time they heard the music come on unassisted, they were asleep in bed at 12:30 a.m. Laurle got up to see what was behind the midnight disturbance. No one was around, as the music played away, clearly and loud.

They say her name is Margaret. She grew up in the big house on the corner and lived there almost all of her life. She never married. Perhaps the young Madison men of her generation whom she would have considered were lost in the First World War. After more than fifty years, Margaret and her sister, Catherine, were the last of their family to live in the home that had been built by their father, Michael Donlan. In a book written in 1922 by A.S. Chapman called *Madison: A Jewel in Setting 'Neath the Hills*, Mr. Donlan is listed as being an owner of the Indiana Foundry. It notes that the business was known to "run with character for fine work and honest dealing nation wide." The Clemenses tell me that Mr. Donlan started the Madison Metals Company. They say that the company provided metal fronts for commercial buildings in Madison and as far away as New Orleans. You can see examples of the work throughout town, but the one example that they mentioned by name, was the front façade on the Attic Coffee Mill Café at 631 West Main Street. The nameplate for Madison Metals is found there, on the metal base of the pilaster. Records from the Jefferson County Library files note that Mr. Donlan, had ties to the banking industry.

Laurle says that Margaret is still there and likes to move things around in the big bedroom on the northeast side. The house was built with nine bedrooms, but that is the one that was Margaret's in her lifetime. She outlived sister Catherine and died there in the house in the 1950s. One can understand why Margaret doesn't want to leave. She seems to feel comfortable in her room. After all, it's been her room for a long time. The owners often feel cold spots in the room that have nothing to do with drafts. Items are also moved around in other rooms of the house. Sometimes they see a bright light that appears and moves across the ceiling. They've looked for reasonable answers

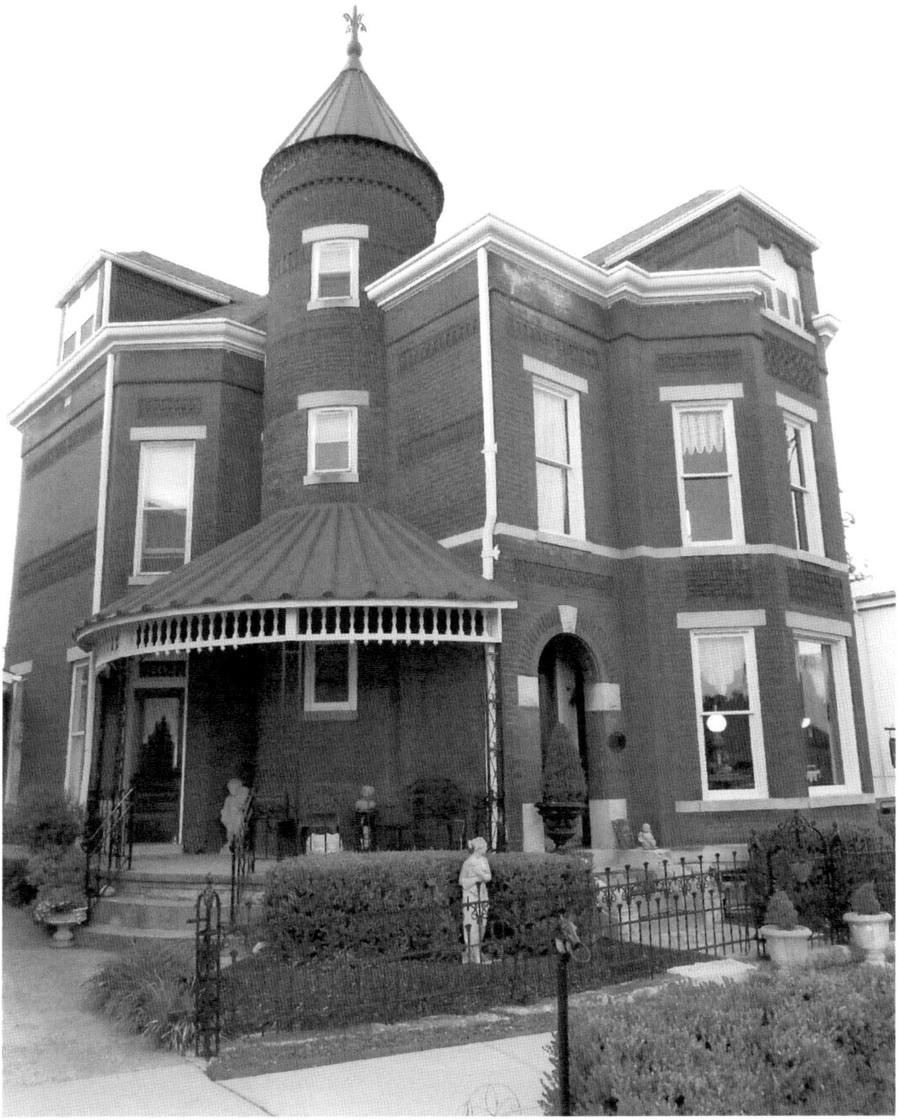

Known as the Donlan House, the huge rambling brick Queen Anne is the scene of a multiple haunting, by one of the Donlan daughters and by priests who boarded at the residence.

for what might cause the appearance of the light, like traffic on the street below or streetlights, but it doesn't look like that and is never something that can be explained away. It appears as an individual light, not connected to other environmental causes.

Laurle, as with others in town who experience ongoing paranormal activity, didn't seem frightened; she is just resigned to the knowledge that she and Ben share their home with several former residents who happen to have passed on.

As long as the CD player that plays the piped music was located in Margaret's bedroom, the music would come on at different times. Ben says that they would be awakened in the middle of the night, with the music playing loudly through the house. It seems that Margaret enjoys turning on the music, and she knows how to work the electronics. That's not unusual for spirits. They appear to learn how to manipulate the technology of paranormal investigators with ease, so why not everyday electronics? The Clemenses outwitted her and moved the CD player to the basement. That solved the problem with the intermittent music playing. Don't tell Margaret where it is!

They had tried to find some background on their home, but it proved to be very elusive. So they were very happy to obtain some detailed information about the family who built their house when they had the opportunity to meet the grandson of the Donlans. He was visiting his family's hometown and doing some research at the Jefferson County Historic Society Museum. It was one of those chance encounters when he happened to meet the very people who lived in the house that his family had built. He was sharing some of his knowledge about the home to people he thought were strangers. The Clemenses were shocked to realize that he was speaking about their own home. He lives in Michigan and is elderly now, but they exchanged information, and he later sent them photos and background about his grandparents and the home.

It turns out that Margaret was his spinster aunt. There were eight children in all, so the parents and each child all had their own bedrooms. Today, there are eight bedrooms, with one of the original having been made into a library. I pulled a title search on the property. It doesn't show the date when the Donlans acquired the property, only when it was sold by the heirs, in 1958. Ben said that there's not much in the records and that no one in town remembers the first owners of the house. But now he has quite a bit of information from their grandson that shows that the Donlans were indeed the first owners.

The house has been in the hands of relatively few owners considering it was built in the late nineteenth century. That is usually a fortunate background for a historic house. It usually means that you will have more original architectural materials intact, which in turn preserves the charming character and historical integrity of a building. It seems that spirits don't like their environments tampered with either, judging by the number of reports of increased paranormal activity when construction is taking place. Reports by homeowners and construction workers show that when changes are made in a spirit-infested building, there are all kinds of objections that occur in the form of moved or hidden tools and loud bangs of protest by the resident ghouls.

As the last Donlan, when Margaret passed, the estate sold the house to the Koczergo family, who were devout Catholics. They had been victims of European concentration camps and were sponsored by the Catholic Church to relocate from Poland to the United States. The family moved into the large home and, in order to assist with finances, took in boarders. The boarders were the young priests serving the local parish.

The sound of footsteps running up and down the stairs is frequently heard in the house, say the couple. Laurle says that she may be on the main floor when she hears someone running, in quick order, up the first flight of stairs, across the hallway and then up the upper stairs. Laurle will sometimes walk over to the stairs when she hears the visitors start their climb. I think she hopes she might catch a look at one of them, but of course, no one is ever there. They're not sure who it is coming and going, but they believe it's possible that it may be the priests who are still on their way to Mass and then returning to their rooms. They don't mind. They feel a sense of "protection" due to the pious tenants. Then again, it could be one of the many children who lived in the house, racing around, as children often do. They never feel threatened by the spirits who obviously inhabit their space. Or is it the other way around? They love sharing their home with the former residents. They say that they are like family.

Indiana's Oldest Hotel

The Broadway Hotel, Restaurant and Tavern

No man is rich enough to buy back his past.
—Oscar Wilde

Madison residents have always heard that there is paranormal activity at the Broadway Hotel, Restaurant and Tavern, but they really have no idea of the great variety of incidents that have been going on in one of Madison's most popular restaurants. It has been featured in the *Chicago Tribune* and *Indianapolis Living* magazine, among other periodicals, with glowing reviews. The business was also listed in *The Haunted Inns of America*, published in 2003, which features one haunted hotel from each state. The Broadway Hotel was chosen to represent the state of Indiana in the book.

The vivacious blonde sat at the table on the patio, obviously comfortable in her environment. She should be. She has been the owner of the establishment for more than twenty years. Before Libby Mann purchased the Broadway Hotel in 1992, she often came to visit Madison and attended the many festivals with her dear friend Brenda, who is a realtor in town. Libby is a trained anesthesiology nurse who just loved the historic downtown, and so on New Year's Eve in 1991, she made up her mind to stay. She asked Brenda to show her some properties that had the potential to make a great bed-and-breakfast. That first week in January, she looked at several properties, but none of them was "just right."

Then, two nights later, as they drove down Broadway, Libby saw the hotel that had a "For Sale" sign posted in front. Even though it was

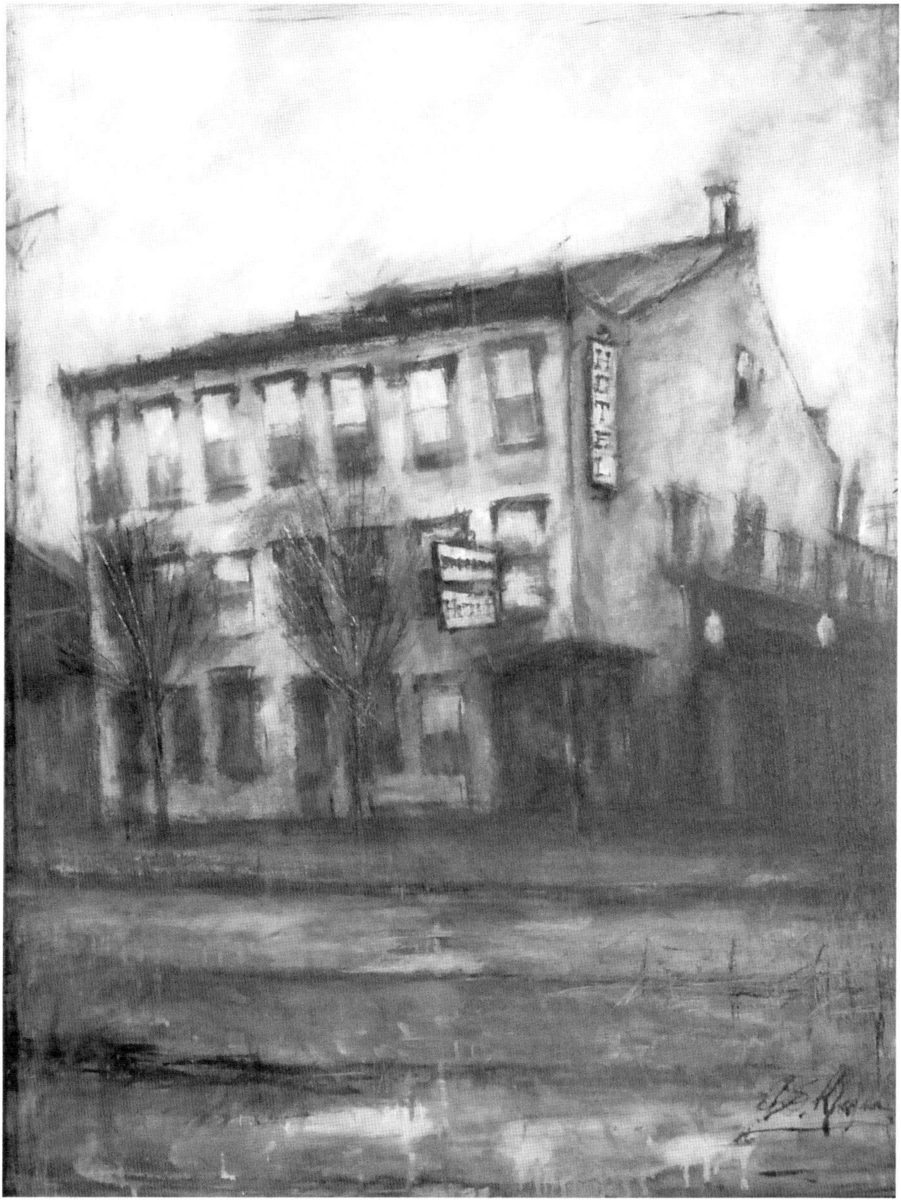

Original painting of the Broadway Hotel, Restaurant and Tavern, by local Madison artist Eric Phagan ©.

8:00 p.m., Libby asked Brenda to call the owner to come there so she could view the property. He came and showed her around the rooms. The building was terribly run-down, but Libby only saw the potential. There are ten rooms on the second floor and ten rooms on the third floor. Every room she looked at was decorated with antique furnishings. Having dealt in antiques, that turned her head. The rooms were being rented for forty dollars per month, and most of the walls and ceilings were painted black, with the exception of one that was decorated with dark velvet flocked wallpaper.

Downstairs, in what is now the lobby, refrigerators and freezers, along with a lawn mower with its parts spread all over the floor, filled the room. The patio, like other rooms of the building, was filled with storage items and was also where the owner kept his dog chained up. Huge pipes ran across the tin ceiling because the bathrooms and steam heat had not been installed until 1901, when instead of pulling the walls apart, the pipes were run along outside the walls and ceiling. The front of the building was painted peach halfway up the wall and white at the top above that. Libby said that some paint cans fell off a truck on I-71 and were on sale for a great price at the paint store. I think that's her way of saying, "What were they thinking!?" In reality, the owner had sent the cook out to paint when business was slow. You could see the roller marks and how tall he was by how far the paint went up the wall.

In spite of the obvious overwhelming challenges, Libby was up to the task. Maurice, the former owner, said that he knew she was going to buy the old building because she could visualize the finished project. As they walked through the showing, she kept saying, "I can put the bar in there and the kitchen here and the tables over there and a fireplace could go here..." When they walked outside, there was a little pink round-topped sign with green printing that read, "The Oldest Hotel in Indiana." Libby asked Brenda, "Is that true?" She could immediately see the marketing potential of that unique designation. Actually, the business started in 1834, next door to the present building, at the corner of Broadway Street and Main Street. During the early twentieth century the business was moved to 313 Broadway Street where it still operates today.

The building had been on the market for five years, so when the offer was presented, it was accepted right away. At the sale closing, the former owners, Peg and Maurice Hublar, said, "You know there's a ghost there. He sits in the second booth and he likes to play the jukebox." I guess they felt like they should disclose that bit of information as they handed over the keys to the old wooden doors. Libby said that she didn't care. She hadn't seen a ghost, and that was the least of her problems at that point. She had never had an experience with the paranormal before.

She went to work, pulling out the modern, undesirable additions to take the inn back in time to a charming dining and gathering spot. While she was working on the project, she lived upstairs in one of the rooms. And strange things did happen in the old building, just as the former owners said they would. As she worked repainting the walls, she would hear whispering, and doors would slam by themselves. Not just one door, but rather the doors to the rooms along the upstairs hallway would slam one after another. She would come back to her room and find that it was unlocked. At first she thought that maybe she had just forgotten to lock it. But it kept happening. She would carefully take notice that she was locking the door but would return later to find that it was again unlocked. She tried to think of a reasonable explanation as to why it would always be unlocked and began to wonder who might have a key to the door.

During the renovation, Libby found some antique beer advertisements in the strangest places. Some were pasted on the tin ceiling and some inside the walls. They are very rare and unique original advertisements from early in the twentieth century, and she had them framed to decorate the pub walls. They look great and enhance the period feeling of the establishment. To highlight the artwork, she purchased high-end battery-run lighting and installed them over the pictures. That was fine for the first hour. When she entered the middle room, she saw that the light over one of the booths was blinking, and there were new batteries in them all. She thought, "Oh great, I'll have to take that one back."

A few nights later, she went upstairs at about 10:00 p.m. to do some work on her computer, with the intention of producing a new menu for the restaurant. Her sister, Kathy, who often works there, was cleaning up downstairs in the bar area. Libby was sitting in a room at the end of a long hallway, with the door open. The stairway is outside the door, on her end of the hall. As she printed off the results of her work, it looked nothing like she expected. Each letter had a different font, and some were even upside down. Being somewhat new to computers, she just thought that something was wrong with the printer. At the other end of the hallway was a basketball on the floor, left there by her sons a few weeks before. As she sat looking at the crazy print of the menu, her eye was drawn to movement out in the hallway. The basketball began to roll down the hall toward her. She just looked at the moving sphere as it came toward her and then turned to roll down the stairs. Bam! Bam! Bam! The ball hit each step, and the sound echoed throughout the building. Libby, shaken by what she had just seen, ran down the stairs into the bar area, where Kathy was just finishing her closing errands. Libby asked her sister, "Did you see that?" She had seen it but also had more to add. "Yeah, I did, and that's not all. I'm down here alone, and the jukebox keeps coming on by itself." But it wasn't playing any of the popular songs of today. It was playing songs that would have been popular during the 1930s—songs that weren't even on the jukebox.

As they stood there, the phone rang, and Kathy picked it up with her usual greeting: "Broadway Tavern." No one was on the other end. She hung up disgusted and said that that was the fifteenth time that phone had rang with no one there. It continued to ring about ten more times in the next half hour, as they finished cleaning. Each time, no one was on the phone.

UNEXPECTED CUSTOMERS

Kathy told Libby about another evening when she was working. A regular who likes to sit at the end of the bar was there nursing his beer. She said that it was nearly closing time, and he was the only customer left in the bar, when the door opened and closed. She heard footsteps move across the floor, and one of the metal barstools scraped the floor as it moved backward. There was the sound of "someone" sitting down on the seat, but there was no one there. The regular looked toward the stool with wide eyes and then back to the bartender. He got up and said something about it being time for him to go, and then he was out the door.

Another of the lady bartenders told about the evening when she was nearly finished with her duties for the night and went to the front door for a breath of air. When she opened the door, a man was walking down the brick sidewalk past the building. It was late, and it caught her off guard. She looked at the man and noticed that he was dressed in a long black coat, a white shirt and a stovetop hat. It was obvious that he was not dressed in average attire. He did not look very friendly, but he didn't stop. He just kept walking, but he turned his head and looked right at her as he walked past. She knew at that moment that he was not of this time. She hurriedly grabbed her purse and ran out of the building.

One of the other employees told about the time the dishes in the kitchen area got the full attention of the staff. The dishes stored on a tall metal storage rack just started shaking for about two minutes, as everyone in the area stopped and stared.

In her third year of ownership, with the renovations still in progress, Libby hired some men to work on the roof. Taking on a 180-year old building takes dedication and perseverance. The weather had cooled, and it was getting near to the time when they were starting to put up the Christmas decorations. It was also time to turn the heat on in the building. They started decorating at the end of November because after having had three years of experience with the decorations, they knew how long it would take to complete the job. Libby said that she would go to the basement with the intention of getting the boxes but would feel fatigued and decide to do it later. Libby began to experience headaches and seemed to be run down. She thought that she was just working too hard. It seemed as though all the employees were working too hard, as well, because they were having the same issues. She purchased a large jar of aspirin for the front desk, and it was empty within a few days.

After going to bed one Friday night, she got up the next morning feeling dizzy, but she had work to do, so she began the tasks of the day. She heard her sister downstairs, at work already. Her sister didn't work on weekends, so Libby went downstairs and asked her what she was doing there. Kathy said that she always comes in on Monday. Libby had slept through the last two days! Realizing that something was very wrong, she called that minute to make a doctor's appointment. When she got off the phone, the lights over the antique advertisements began blinking. And not just one light, but all of them, in sequence of three blinks at a time, a pause and then three blinks again. Next, the jukebox began to play some strange music that sounded like the prelude to a suspense show. It just played for about fifteen seconds and then stopped. It seemed as though the spirit in the building was demanding to be noticed.

She took the lights back to the store in which she had purchased them and told the salesperson that they didn't work. As she laid the lights out on the counter to demonstrate what she meant, the lights never blinked one time. They worked perfectly. Libby said, "I'm sorry, I just can't use these." She didn't say why they didn't work for her. She left out the part about the ghost who likes to play with them.

OUIJA ANSWERS

After the months of harassment, Libby had to accept the reality of a spirit inhabiting her building. She wanted answers, now. So she attacked the problem face on and did the only thing she could think of to get those answers. She went to the store and purchased a Ouija board. She didn't know how it worked or if it would work, but she took it home, called a girlfriend over to help and started asking questions.

She said it was surprising how fast the planchette (the three-legged stool) began to move all over the board, answering her questions swiftly and definitely. She asked, "Is there a spirit here?" Yes came the first answer. "What is your name?" she inquired. The planchette moved to the C, followed by H…A…R…L…E…S…M…O…R…G…A…N. The question-and-answer session continued.

"Did you live here?" No.

"Where did you live?" Chicago.

"What was your work?" Liquor.

"When did you die?" 1930.

"Did you die here?" No.

"Where did you die?" French Lick.

"How did you die?" Shot.

"Who did you work for?" The boys.

"Were you married?" No.

"Were you in love?" Yes.

"Why didn't you marry her?" Money.

"Is she here?" Yes.

"Why are you here?" Fun.

Do you have something to tell me? For the next ten minutes, the planchette kept going to C and then to the O, over and over again. She didn't know what that meant at that time. She thought that maybe it was an abbreviation for "company." She wondered what that might mean.

Libby had scheduled an appointment with the doctor to look into the ongoing headaches and came down in the morning ready to go. But she stopped suddenly in the kitchen because she smelled natural gas. It smelled very strong. She picked up the phone, called the gas company and said she thought she had a gas leak. They come pretty quickly when they get those reports, so the company sent its inspector right away. He started to measure the air with a tester. It beeped loudly and continuously.

The inspector informed her that there was a carbon monoxide leak and told her to get everyone out of the building. They found that when the workmen had been on the roof, they had knocked some bricks down the chimney that has the exhaust pipes installed, and they had blocked the airflow. He said what had saved them was the airflow from the windows and the building construction. Old buildings were constructed to have airflow in a time before modern cooling and heating technologies. They made the repairs and left Libby and her employees in a much healthier environment.

Libby knew that all the frantic signs that had been occurring in the building lately were Charlie's way of warning her that something was terribly wrong. She later thought about that message on the Ouija board. It kept pointing to C and O, and the chemical formula for carbon dioxide is CO_2. She realized that Charlie was looking out for her, and she started to give more thought to the answers he had given to her that night. She had a good idea of what had happened to him. Charlie had said that his business had been "liquor" and that he was employed by "the boys." She deduced that he was a member of the mob and had been shot at the mobsters' favorite resort in Indiana, French Lick. Since the turn of the century, the famous and infamous came for the illegal casino gambling, an ill-kept secret allowed to flourish thanks to a politically well-connected promoter.

And who was the woman he loved but didn't marry because of money? Libby said that she may have been related to one of the affluent families of Madison. Charlie would have made big money in the liquor business in the late '20s and early '30s during prohibition. But *her* family's money was the reason they couldn't get married. They were at the top of the social order. Her family would never have approved of their relationship. He was a bad boy and she was a princess of society. Libby said that she has not investigated their existence—she knows it is so and doesn't need to see it on paper to prove it.

After the incident with the carbon monoxide, Libby did give the Ouija board another try to get a few more answers. She knew that Charlie's antics were warnings about the poisonous gas and was grateful to him. She thanked him for trying to take care of her and asked him if he liked her sister, Kathy. "Ohhh, yeah!" came the answer. "Do you like me?" she asked. "I love you."

It's Good to Have Otherworldly Friends

She had an opportunity to test that declaration soon after that. She had planned a trip with some friends to the Bahamas and was really looking forward to getting away. Just before she left, she opened some mail and was shocked to see a telephone bill for $2,000. She couldn't believe it, but there it was. She was upset but would have to address it later because it was time to leave for the airport. When they reached the Bahamas, they were warned that a hurricane was coming and were given a candle and told to fill the bathtub with water. The storm hit very quickly, and for several days, they didn't have any power. It was not exactly the vacation that they had planned. The power finally came back on the day they were going to fly home. They had an opportunity to go to the casino across the street for one hour before they had to leave for the airport. Libby thought, "Charlie, you're good at gambling; help me win the $2,000 for that phone bill." She only had an hour, but she sat down at a table and, with just a few hands of poker, was winning! The more she played, the more she won. At the end of the hour, she walked away with $2,200. I guess it is good to have a Charlie.

When she got home, her friend Vern heard about Charlie helping her in the casino and joked with her, saying that he wanted to take Charlie with him to Las Vegas. She spoke to Charlie and said, "Okay, Charlie, I know you would love to go to Las Vegas, so go and have a good time, but be sure you come back." She got a call the next day from Vern. He had won $23,000.

Madison has a fantastic juried Chautauqua Art Festival every year during the last weekend of September. The town swells with up to seventy thousand happy visitors. Every business in town is overflowing with guests, and the Broadway Tavern is one of the most popular. It sits half a block from the festival entrance so it is a great place to go and relax for a drink or a meal in a fun, historic atmosphere. A few years ago, some ladies from Cincinnati came in and were having a wonderful time. Libby was acting as hostess when one of the ladies pulled her aside, told her that she was a psychic and said, "You know, there are many entities in this place. Young and old, men and women. Yes, you have ghosts." Well, that was not really news to Libby by that point.

On another occasion, a lady came in by herself for lunch, and Libby led her down the middle patio aisle and got about halfway down the length of the room. The lady then stopped her and said, "I'm sorry, I'm going to have to go someplace else," and then turned to head back the way that they had

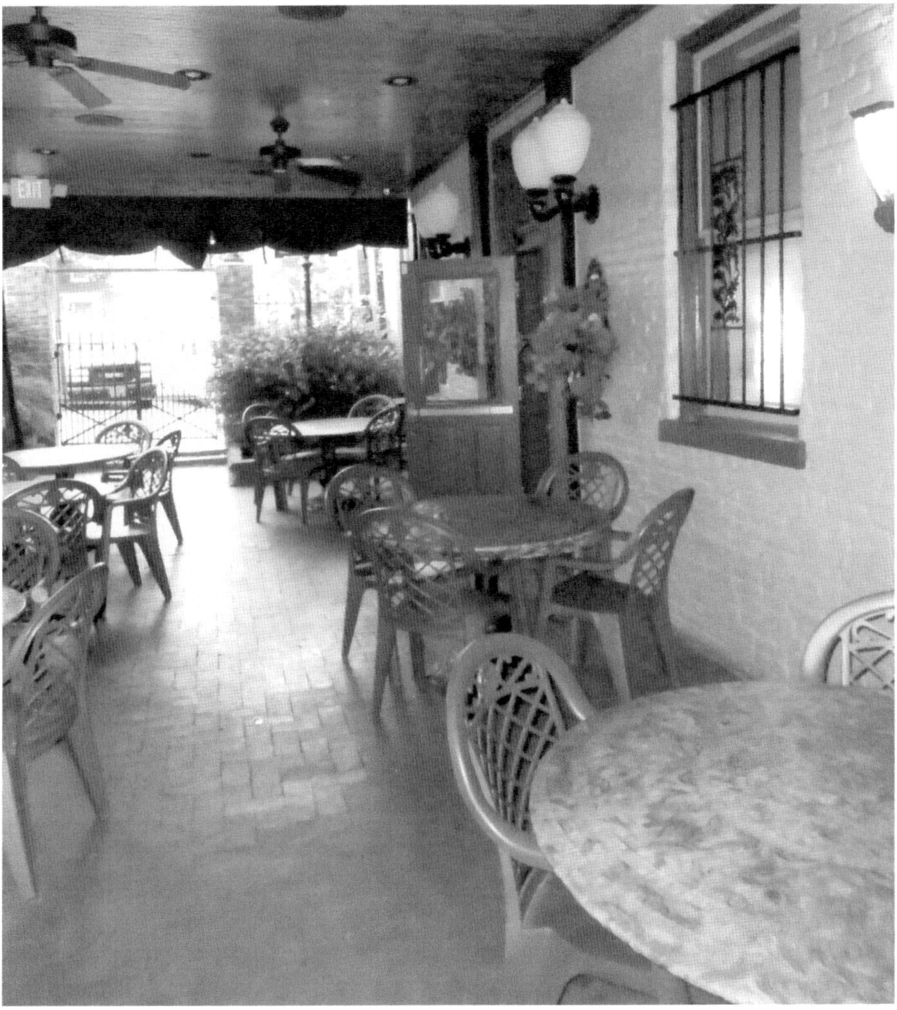

The patio of the Broadway Restaurant may look empty, but you never know when someone from the past will pull out a chair and sit down with you.

just come. Libby, surprised by the sudden turnaround, said, "Is something wrong?" The lady said, "I'm psychic, and there are a bunch of people inside having a party and drinking and dancing. They're dressed in clothes from the past—from about a hundred years ago. I can see them through the window [of the patio into the dining room]. The room is from another time, too. I just want to eat in peace. I'm sorry, I just can't eat here." And with that, she exited through the front iron gate.

Ghost in the Mirror

In 2011, Libby hired a female decorator and her son to do some work upstairs in one of the rooms. They came at all hours to work, and one late evening, the woman was removing wallpaper in a bedroom. As she worked, she watched TV, but through the mirror because her back was to the screen. As she worked and watched, she suddenly saw a woman appear in the mirror, in the room with her. She had blond hair in an up-do and was dressed in Edwardian style, with a white, high-necked, long-sleeved blouse and a long dark skirt—like what you would expect to see at the turn of the nineteenth century. Balanced on her fingertips was a silver tray, carried high in the air, and as the decorator watched, she smiled at her, turned and twirled around with a swift movement and went out the door. The decorator turned to look at the door, but no one was there. She ran out of the room and asked her son, who was working in the hall, if he had seen anyone come out the door and into the hallway, and of course he hadn't.

Word gets around when you have a building full of spirits, and the reports have gone on for decades. So it was no surprise that Libby would get calls from paranormal investigation groups requesting an opportunity to explore her hotel. She agreed to let them come. She said that she was surprised at all the equipment that they bring with them. Cameras, recorders, energy measuring instruments that blinked and lots of wires. Two different groups have come from Indianapolis, one from a local county group, and they both filmed their experiences. They came and set up a little after midnight, right after closing time. Libby stayed to observe their findings. She sat at the bar watching TV as they moved around the rooms, calling out to the spirits. They came into the bar area and asked, "If there is anyone here, knock three times." Libby said that they asked that same question over and over for the next thirty minutes. Finally, she said, "Do you want me to try?" They seemed skeptical but said yes anyway. She said, "Charlie, knock three times." And he did! The group members' eyes got huge, and they all got very excited. Charlie and his companions did not disappoint the guests. By the time they left, the investigators had told her that there is one male ghost in the tavern room and a woman and a man in the back dining rooms, possibly the same man as in the tavern. By that time, Libby was fully aware of her unseen residents.

A couple once made reservations to stay at the hotel a few weeks after Christmas. The wife had given her husband a book about the *Haunted Inns*

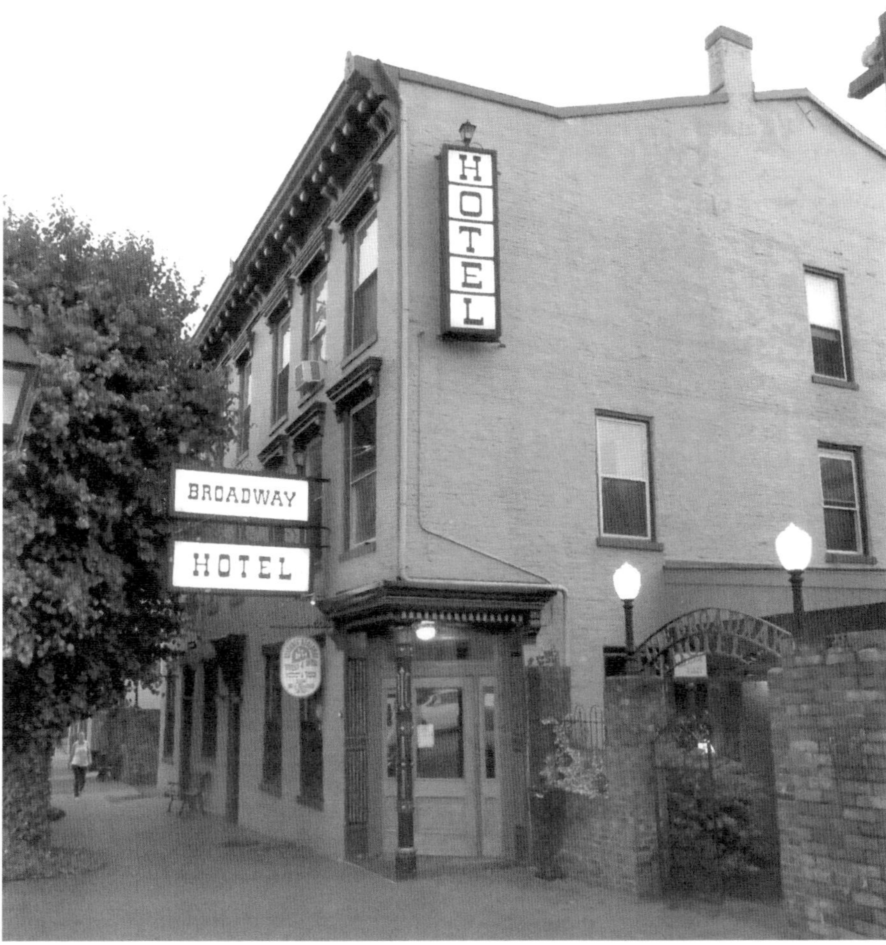

Broadway Hotel, Restaurant and Tavern, where the living and the dead come for a good time.

of America, and they were going to try to visit each one that was listed. They chose the Broadway for their first stop.

Recently, a friend of Libby's took a digital photo in the middle tavern room. When he looked at it, there was a foggy mass floating in the air, with a face seemingly in the middle of it. Looks as though Charlie likes to have his picture taken.

Old hotels reverberate with the memories of the past. It's little wonder that so many hotels are haunted. Today, the Broadway Hotel, Restaurant and Tavern is a favorite site in town. It has two dining rooms inside, an outdoor patio under cover and a bar area, also with two rooms. The sound of music is heard drifting from the back of the patio, where live performers often play. The restaurant fills every night with hungry patrons and folks who just want to have a good meal and a good time. They don't mind sharing their table with the others. They probably won't even notice the presence of the unearthly inhabitants, who after all are just there for a little fun, too.

THE KITCHEN SHADOW

Nothing in the universe can travel at the speed of light, they say,
forgetful of the shadow's speed.
—Howard Nemerov

317 West Third Street

In April 2011, I attended a state preservation conference in Indianapolis and stayed at the beautiful and historic Columbia Club on Monument Circle. It has a fantastic history involving two political parties. It used to be the club of only the Republican Party, with the Democratic Party's club being just down the street. After a fire destroyed the Democrats' club, they began to share the same building that the Republicans had previously used alone. Apparently, there are many stories of scandalous behavior taking place at the club. If those walls could tell us their stories, what would they say?

While at the conference, I ran into an old friend. She caught me up on what was new in her life. One of the most interesting things that she shared was that she had become involved with a paranormal investigation group. I told her that I was writing a book about the ghosts of Madison. During the conversation, she said that my accommodations were rumored to be haunted. I admitted that I did get a bit of a "feeling" in my room. Anyway, after returning home from the conference, I had another busy day, but that didn't stop me from one of my favorite pastimes—staying up late and working on my computer. Well, let me share what I wrote to my friend about that night. The following is what I wrote to her the week after my return home:

> *It was 3:30 A.M. and I was sitting at my kitchen table, working on my laptop computer, when I saw a movement that was obvious enough to distract me from the screen. First, I saw it in the large ceiling to floor multi-pained window, facing me, to the left side of the room. Then, in the panes of the door which was directly across from me, as though someone had moved across the room from the left side, to the right side. I thought, maybe someone is outside. I didn't see anyone. Suddenly, one of my pug dogs, 10 year old Rumple, started barking, which he has never done, before or after this, in the middle of the night, and it made me jump. His hair was raised up on his back in alarm, as thought a stranger had entered the house. I was unnerved, and scolded him; "Shhhh, stop it." It seemed very loud, since it was early morning, and the rest of the house was quiet. I now know that*

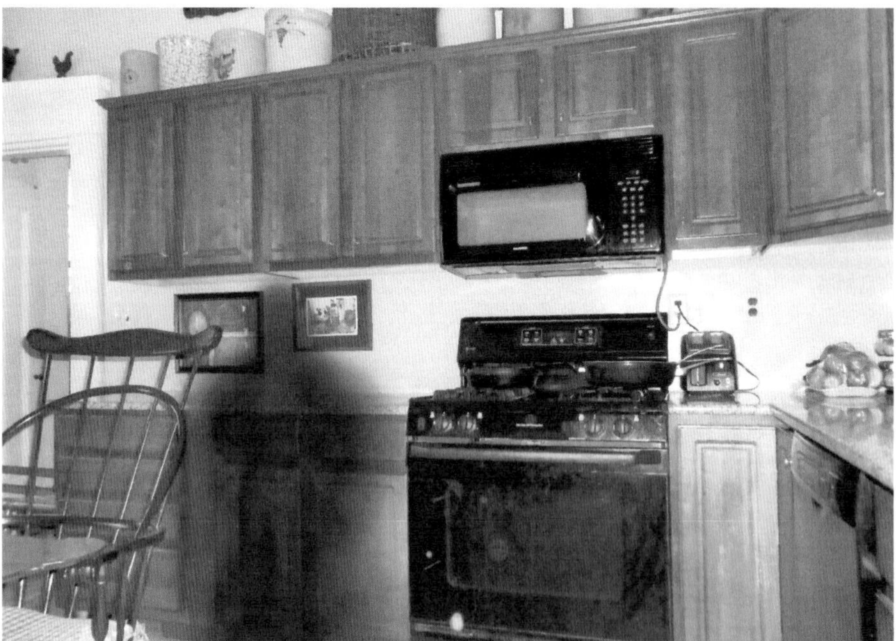

The kitchen at 317 West Third Street. This image shows the location of the shadow person sighting and caught the glowing anomalies in front of the stove that are believed to be a manifestation of the owner's pet pug dog Winston, who passed in 2010. She often feels him brush by her legs in the kitchen as he did in life. *Image enhancement by Barbie Guitard Canipe.*

dogs have been recognized, as being sensitive to ghosts. But some experienced investigators say that it is not that they see an apparition, but that they are sensitive to the electromagnetic and air pressure changes, that are known to accompany the presence of poltergeist. I don't know which is correct, but Rumple knew someone or something was there.

I tried to ignore it and continued to work on my computer. A few minutes later out of the corner of my eye I saw it...a thick, blackest of black, shadow. It started out right next to me and moved down the side of my kitchen, past the stove and down the length of the long, granite countertop. As I looked up and straight on to that area, nothing was there, but I knew that something had just been there. Strangely, I was not afraid, even though I knew what it was. I returned to my computer screen and tried to get the thoughts that were running through my head to go away. As though, if I ignored it, then it would go away. A few minutes later, I began to feel something touching me at my side, poking me and tugging at the bottom of my shirt. I shifted in my chair. Again, I tried to ignore it, but it continued to

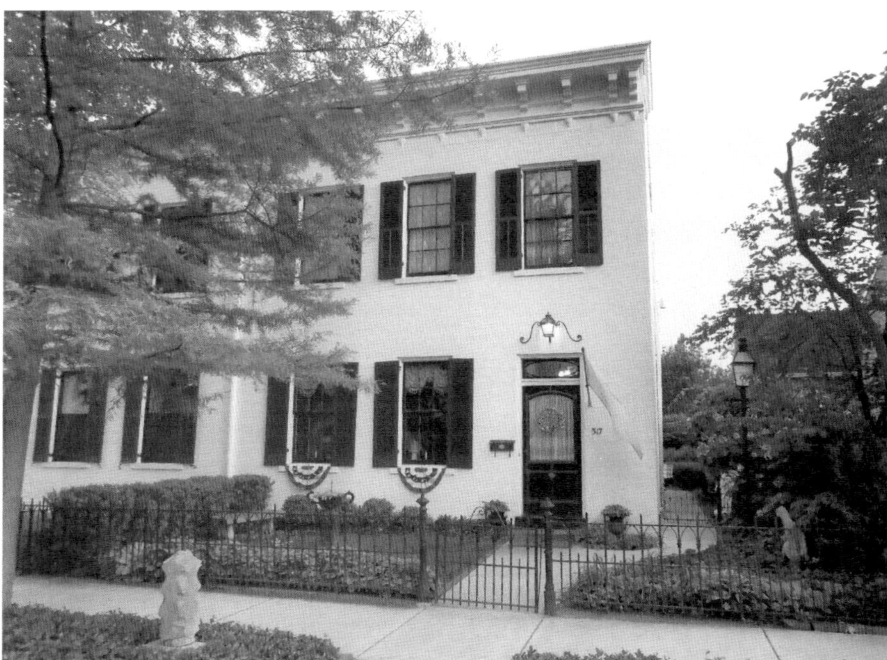

Home of the author at 317 West Third Street. Known as a double house, it is a form similar to other rowhouse-type buildings. At least four deaths have occurred in the house when the White family lived here over a period of eighty years.

poke at me. I have always had a belief in the presence of spirits, but hoped that I would never experience them in my own home. I thought that I would be terrified. And here it was happening now. I was very surprised and a bit unsettled, but not "terrified." It just didn't seem to feel threatening to me.

A few more pokes at my side and I said "Ok, that's it." I decided that I had, had enough and got up to go to bed, not wishing to tempt fate. Nothing bad had really happened up to that point, except a little interaction with one of the shadow people, and I didn't want to push my luck. I guarantee that I moved a little faster and looked over my shoulder all the way to my bedroom on the second floor.

The next morning, my husband had gotten up early, as usual. When he came back in the bedroom to get dressed, he said "I think we have ghosts." I jumped straight up and said "I know!" He had clearly heard someone walking down the upstairs hall, while he was downstairs. He thought it was me, until he came upstairs and saw that I was asleep in bed. I told him what I had experienced the night before. We both wondered what had prompted this appearance.

That is the only time that I have had that experience at my own house. Maybe the spirit was just passing through. But it really confirmed that this 'presence' wanted to be known to us at that exact time. Maybe one of the Columbia Club spirits just wanted a change in scenery and had followed me home.

The Main Street Laundress

There are an infinite number of universes existing side by side and through which our consciousnesses constantly pass. In these universes, all possibilities exist. You are alive in some, long dead in others, and never existed in still others. Many of our "ghosts" could indeed be visions of people going about their business in a parallel universe or another time—or both.
—*Paul F. Eno,* Faces at the Window

322 West Main Street

Today, the charming building at 322 West Main is composed of a working shop on the bottom floor and living quarters above. Mike Totten, who is trained as a professional architect, uses the shop to support his businesses of long rifle making and refurbishing treadle sewing machines. People walking by on the sidewalk are drawn into the building by the delightful period-style displays in the large, multipaned window and by his friendly, open-door policy. You will find him on any given day sitting outside, demonstrating his skill of carving a block of wood into a pistol stock or a working period-style long rifle that doubles as a stunning piece of art. There is a great demand and much-deserved appreciation for his pieces. He enjoys the teaching aspect of his work and shares his knowledge of the craft freely. Upon entering the first room on the main floor, you are surrounded by working treadle sewing machines of all makes, sizes and wood cabinet types. He refurbishes the sewing machines and sells them in the engaging setting. It is a kind of museum/salesroom hybrid.

And he will enthusiastically share the history of the self-powered marvels with anyone who asks.

When it was built in 1847 as the Schecter family home, they had no way of knowing that it would stay in the family for 167 years. It underwent several architectural changes during that time. The entrance was moved from the alley side on the east to the Main Street side on the south, to what is now the front of the building. What is now known as Main Street, up until the 1880s, was called Main Cross. When this house was being built, the golden age of Madison had taken hold, and a building boom was in full swing. This area was being developed, with buildings popping up in quick succession. The building spree spread from the center of the town between East and West Streets to the west and north of town.

By 1964, Mrs. Jones, the last member of the family to live in the house, had passed away. Then it was sold and converted into five multi-family apartments on the two floors. At about the same time, the buildings surrounding 322 West Main suffered the same sorrowful consequence.

Mike purchased the building in 1993 and worked on it while he still lived an hour to the northwest in Columbus, Indiana. He worked on it for two days a week to restore it from the multi-family apartment complex back to a single-family residence/business. This would have been a common usage when the building was erected. Many of the buildings all over town housed family living quarters on upper floors and conducted various businesses out of a front or back room on the main floor.

Sometimes, the frustration of dealing with uneven walls and pealing plaster would erode Mike's usual good nature and drive him to take a break from the current aggravation. During those times, he would find himself drawn to one particular area, in the southeast corner of the front room. It is positioned by a window that looks out at Main Street. He would sit by the window and feel a calm come over him, releasing the latest irritation. It seemed as though the air was cleaner there. He could only describe it as "fresh and calming."

On one occasion, he had taken a break in his favorite corner and was getting ready to go back to work when he heard a faint disturbance by the stair bottom, which raises from the central, east side of the house. He couldn't identify the nature of the noise—maybe it was a scratching sound? Curious, he walked over to the spot and looked up and around the stairs. He saw sparkling dust particles floating in the air, backlit by his work lamp, creating the look of tiny snowflakes. Suddenly, he felt a *whoosh* of cold air with such a force that his hair blew back away from his face. Shocked by

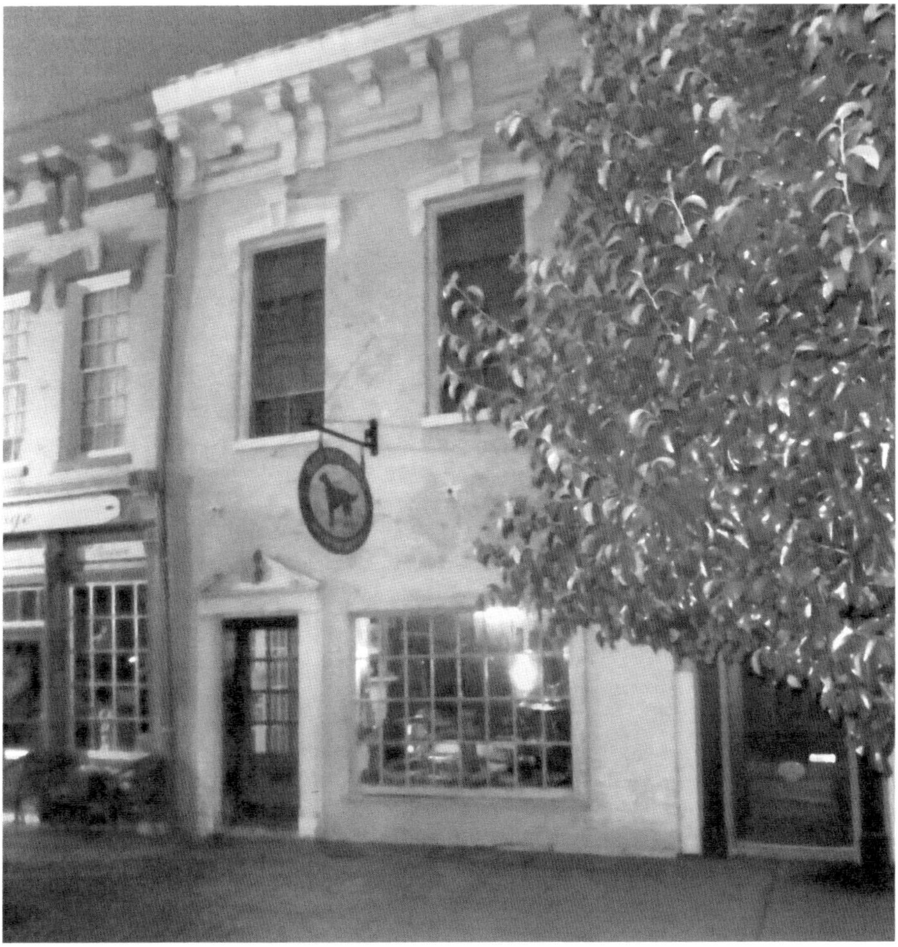

Red Dog Antiques at 322 West Main Street. The laundress is often seen in the front street-level window.

being more or less hit in the face by whatever it was, he ran through the front door and out of the house. As he regained his composure, he thought about the last few minutes and recalled the menacing feeling of an evil presence. That seemed to be what had prompted him to vacate the building so quickly, as if he sensed it was something very bad. Whatever it was, it didn't seem to like Mike's messing with "its" environment. Mike decided that he had done enough work for that evening and retired for the night. But it wouldn't be the last time that he got that feeling by the stairs. He continued to feel cold spots there, as well as the sense that something or someone not so nice was stationed there, critiquing the progress on the project.

On one occasion, Mike had brought his wife and seven-year-old son, Shawn, along with him on a weekend "camp out" in the house. While the couple slept in a Dutch bed, Shawn slept in a hammock in one of the other upstairs bedrooms. When they got up, Shawn asked his dad what he had been doing earlier that morning. Mike asked him, "What do you mean?" Shawn explained that he had gotten up to go down the hall to the bathroom, and as he passed by his parents' room, he said that he saw his dad sitting cross-legged on the bed, looking toward the hall. Mike asked what he looked like. Shawn said he looked like his dad, but he had on a black jacket and white shirt, with a round hat. And he looked really mad. Mike tucked that piece of information away in his head, not wanting to scare his young son with what he thought it was. But every time he later asked Shawn to recite his remembrance about the incident, he told him the same story of the grumpy man wearing the derby hat.

That's not the only spirit thought to inhabit the second floor. Mike says that there is the spirit of a dog there and that he sometimes feels the dog brush by and against him. The dog is not one of his two Irish setters, Pal or Piper. Customers have mentioned that they feel an unseen dog rub by their legs, too. He doesn't see the phantom dog, but Piper will sit and stare at the corner for hours, as though his ghost dog friend is sitting there entertaining him with unseen tricks.

While Mike made progress on restoring the home, the then middle-aged grandchildren of the former owner would stop in at various times to see the changes he was making in the building. As he worked pulling out newer drywall, he uncovered a fireplace that had been hidden for an unknown number of years. When one of the grandsons saw it, he yelled at Mike, asking why he had installed a fireplace there. Mike gently explained that he had not installed it but had discovered it when removing non-original walls.

The three grandchildren of the last owner of the house had been raised there by Grandmother Jones. When they would stop in, they would tell Mike stories about living with her there during the 1930s. He also found out about the corner where he liked to sit by the window. Apparently, Grandmother Jones took in laundry to help support the family during the meager years of the Great Depression. She would set up her big wash pan in the southeast corner—the very corner that Mike found so calming. These were the answers behind the clean, fresh smell of that spot—the scent of soap and fresh laundry. A grandson gave Mike a photograph of his grandmother hanging laundry on the clothesline located on the back roof of the house.

He also gave Mike a photo of the pilot of the *City of Madison*, a side-wheeler paddleboat, standing in the backyard of the house. The pilot, who was a Madison man, had been a good friend of the family and often stopped by to visit and tell his tales of traveling on the river. The *City of Madison* had fifty-eight staterooms and had been built in 1882 by Madison Marine Ways. The boat was owned by the U.S. Mail Line Company and ran from Cincinnati to Madison and from Cincinnati to Louisville. The ill-fated riverboat later struck the Madison Dike and sank in 1894, just east of Madison on the Ohio River. All of this bears out the old river tradition that the most dangerous spot in the world for a pilot is that stretch of the river where he was born and raised.

One morning, not long after hearing the story of Mrs. Jones, Mike descended the stairs to get ready for his day's work. Energy doesn't disappear, but it can be transformed in some way. The energy of many years of work in that corner still lingers to this day. Oftentimes the smells long associated with activities that took place at some intersection of the past may suddenly drift into the nostrils of the unsuspecting.

As he moved down the stairs to the lower level, he began to smell the scent of fresh laundry hovering in the air. His eyes immediately went toward the front corner of the building, by the front window. The first things he noticed were the lights and shadows playing on the ceiling. As his eyes moved downward, he looked through a haze and realized that standing there was the misty form of an elderly lady leaning over a tub, her arms moving up and down in a motion like that of scrubbing clothes on a washboard. He could see that she wore a full apron over her short-sleeved, 1930s-style dress, and her hair was worn up at the back of her head in a bun. Shocked by the sight of someone found unexpectedly in the room, he stopped on the bottom stair and just stood there, trying to gather his bearings and figure out how she had gotten in there. Wanting to get a closer look, he cautiously stepped onto the floor and walked toward the vision without taking his eyes off her. As he walked toward her, she seemed to become aware of him, because she turned around and looked at him, and as she did, she suddenly disappeared. The misty aura that had surrounded her was gone, and in its place was the morning sunlight coming through the front window. Since then, Mike has seen Mrs. Jones several times. He realized who she was from the photograph of her hanging laundry on the clothesline at the back of the house. She is a remnant of the past caught up in repeating the long labors of her time.

He doesn't mind her presence; in fact, he welcomes it. He knows when she is going to appear by the fresh scent of clean laundry in the air. And with the completion of the restoration, the malicious poltergeist has not been heard from again. The cold spots are gone, and so is the uncertain feeling of dread. Maybe that one is satisfied with the job that Mike has done on "his" building.

Mike wrote me an e-mail to tell me about his most recent experience. He was heating up something in the microwave the other evening when he saw a movement in the glass window of the door. He looked up and could see the "grumpy man" in the reflection of the glass. He said, "He does look like me!" He stood there and looked at Mike for a moment and then turned around and left the room through the door. It seems that the inhabited buildings may remain quiet for periods of time, but you never know when they will be showing up again. I think he is just keeping track of what is going on in the building. It's just hard to say what he is so grumpy about. And everyone is grumpy once in a while.

Little John James Lanier

The lawn
Is pressed by unseen feet, and ghosts return
Gently at twilight, gently go at dawn,
The sad intangible who grieve and yearn…
—T.S. Eliot

Vernon Drive

Although, it was a cloudy day on April 20, 1836, the rain that had plagued the region for days had finally stopped. But the gloom of the day soon paled in comparison to the dark cloud about to descend over the town.

It is unclear where the Lanier family lived before they lived in their big mansion that overlooks the Ohio River, built between 1843 and 1844. Many think that they lived in a brick house that used to sit on the southwest corner at Elm and First.

Mr. and Mrs. Lanier are known to have had numerous indentured servants who served in various capacities throughout the house. They had taken in young people and unfortunates who came from difficult economic situations, and the purses helped the families of the indentured. The contractual duration for most indentured servants was to last until the age of twenty-one. The family coachman, Elisha, was described as a "Dwarf Negro boy" and was employed by Mr. Lanier.

Elisha hooked up the finest horses in town to the finest coach, proud to be driving for Mr. Lanier. At this juncture, the story becomes confusing.

Some believe that, one day, Mr. Lanier drove to the bank by himself, only to be interrupted during the workday with news of a terrible accident: the coachman had driven into the river to give the horses a drink of water, and they were drawn into a whirlpool. Another version notes that Lanier's sons—Alexander, sixteen years old, and John James, not quite seven years old, along with cousin Oliver Sheets—had accompanied him in the carriage that day.

That version goes like this. The boys had jumped into the coach, eager for a change of scenery after being cooped up inside during the many rainy days of the past week. Their hair blew in the April breeze as they smiled and laughed with enthusiastic anticipation. Their father had business to take care of at the Indiana National Bank and, seeing their excitement, allowed the boys to accompany him on the ride through town. As Mr. Lanier worked at the bank, the boys played, running along the sidewalk and annoying the patrons trying to enter the Mercantile owned by Oliver's father on the corner of Main Cross and Mulberry, two doors down from the bank. When Mr. Lanier came out of the bank, he called to the boys to return to the coach to begin the ride home. According to the local newspaper of the day, the *Indiana Republican*, on June 21, "He asked Elisha to take the carriage to the River and give it a good washing to remove the dirt and mud from the streets of Madison. (He couldn't have mud on the wheels of the best coach in town.) Elisha wanted to take the boys back home (then at the corner of Elm and First) but the boys wanted to go to the River with him."

Elisha eased the horses down the embankment toward the river at the levy between West Street and Mulberry. The abundant rainfall had swollen the river, and although the water had receded somewhat, it still rushed and rolled along the banks. Not realizing the overpowering strength of the engorged river, Elisha drove the carriage into the water. It was thought at the time that they were caught in "a drop off and an Eddy, or a whirlpool-like current." The horses struggled to keep their balance, but the rushing waters quickly overtook them. The weight of the carriage they were harnessed to prevented their escape and ensured their doom. As it began to overturn, Elisha jumped from the vehicle along with the two Lanier boys and Oliver, who were now struggling for their lives in the pulling, sucking waters. The two older boys, Alexander and Oliver, made it to the shore, coughing and sputtering. They turned to see the horrible sight of the carriage and horses being carried away down the churning river. As their wits came back to them, they realized that little John James and Elisha had not made it to the riverbank, and they could not see them in the river. Panic and shock spurred them to their feet, and they rushed toward the house screaming for Mrs. Lanier. It took several weeks before little John James's lifeless body was found downstream in the river. Sadness overtook the city as the story spread of the little boy who went out for an adventure but ended in tragedy. The paper reported it as a heartbreak "to the family of both the Laniers and family and friends of Elisha."

It is difficult to know when the sightings of a phantom child began to surface. The first known accounts were reported in the 1970s when joggers thought that they saw a young boy in the early morning fog walking up the bank from the river. Wondering what parent would allow their child out alone at such an unlikely time, the joggers ran toward the child only to have him disappear as they came near.

Many people take part in a cool walk along the river in the evening. A little boy has been seen coming up from the river and crossing the road in the evening. One thing is certain. The tale of the little ghost boy is one of the better-known hauntings in town.

The Lady in Red

We make trifles of terrors, ensconcing ourselves into seeming knowledge, when we should submit ourselves to an unknown fear.
—Shakespeare

511 West First Street

You now know the story of the Lanier Mansion, near where little John James Lanier is seen moving from the river looking for his mother, but there is more to the story. There is another who wanders the grounds, unable to rest in peace.

Visitors to the State Landmark Historic Site love to see inside the huge rooms of the mansion, whose riverside entrance is punctuated by the thirty-foot pillars on the fifty-foot-wide portico. Groups travel through the building and are told the stories of the period furnishings and the tales of the former owners. Annual programs are scheduled, enticing visitors back to the grounds year after year. The house museum holds garden plant exchanges, children's preservation activities, afternoon teas, Civil War reenactments and, the most popular events, the Halloween holiday programs. The much anticipated and well-attended "Night Spirits" program, with an adults-only storytelling tour one evening, ends with light refreshments in the spooky basement of the mansion. On another evening, the children attend the "Spooky Mansion" program on the grounds, which come alive with Civil War "ghosts" portrayed by local reenactors, shooting long rifles and reliving

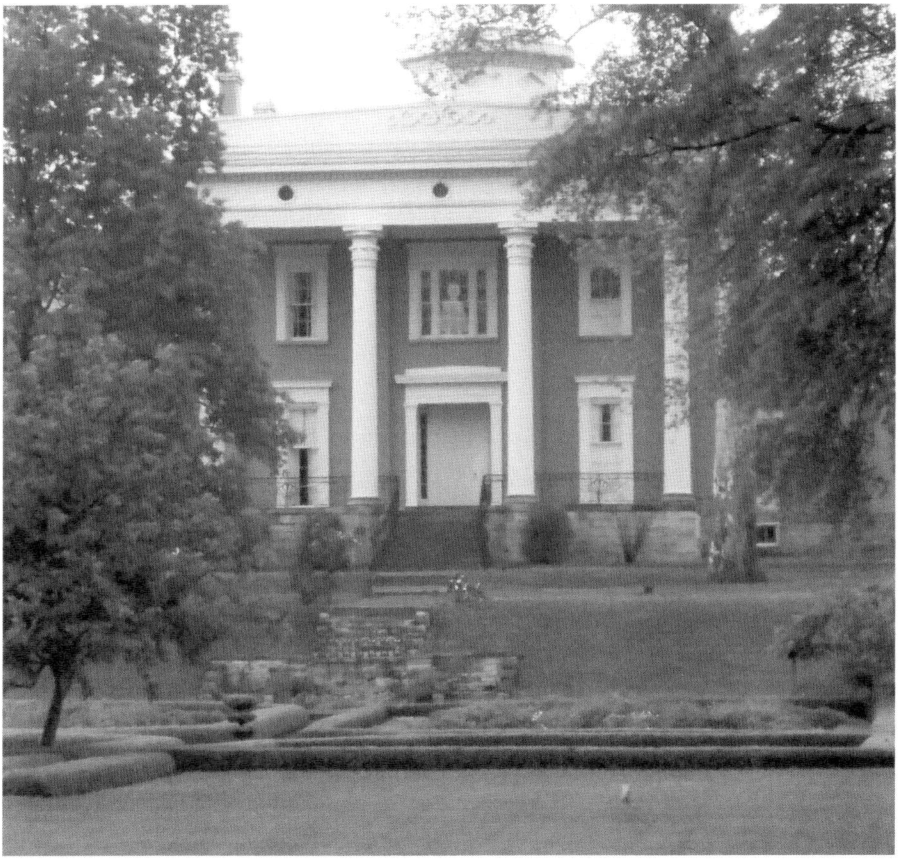

Lanier Mansion, a State Historic Landmark and home of the Lady in Red. People who have caught glimpses of her are most frequently on the second or third floor. *Image enhancement by Barbie Guitard Canipe.*

the War Between the States. Some younger children are frightened by the loud blasts of the black powder guns, but most delight in the scene, tugging on parents' sleeves to come watch the portrayal in the smoke-filled darkness. Squeals of delight and "ooohs" of surprise are heard with each blast of the guns shot by the military men depicting Rebels and Yankees.

Inside, actors and volunteers tell stories along the tour route to the groups that move through the building during the evening events. Several have told of the sighting of a mysterious period-dressed woman moving around on the upper floors.

Arguably the best-known ghost tale in town is about the Lady in Red. Her identity, though, is not so certain. She has been seen by tour guides, reenactors, guests and tourists, who often ask about the woman in period dress. At first, some think that she's one of the docents. Then they notice other details. They become conscious of the fact that she is not of this world, as she seems to "float" above the floor. She wears a long, floor-length red dress. Perhaps when her spirit was released from her body, she found herself in a familiar setting and decided to stay. Women in red, along with women in white, are often seen in places known to be haunted. Both are thought to be looking for something or someone, mourning or distressed.

The big house that overlooks the Ohio River was built as the home of James F.D. Lanier. It is a magnificent Greek Revival jewel declared by wealthy visitors of the nineteenth century to be as fine as any found in Cincinnati or Louisville. The architect was Francis Costigan, and although his beautiful designs are found throughout town, this is his most acclaimed work.

Lanier came to Madison as a young man of seventeen with his mother and father, both of whom saw opportunity in the wild early settlement. Two years later, in 1819, he married a beautiful girl named Elizabeth Gardner. She was two years his senior and born in Virginia, more recently of Lexington, Kentucky, where her father was a town leader. Elizabeth was described by all as an intelligent and charming woman who had her choice of husbands. James's family believed that she "had breeding that would maintain the family stature." While James and Elizabeth raised their children in the house, we believe that the third floor was used by the younger children, for guests and for storage. The rooms on that floor are six feet, four inches high and have round windows for light. In contrast, the first floor has fourteen-foot ceilings and the second floor has twelve-foot ceilings.

Their agreeable union bore eight children and lasted twenty-seven years, ending with her death at the age of forty-eight. She passed away in the winter and was laid out in the parlor of the mansion before being moved to the vault to wait until the frozen ground thawed enough for burial. She was buried at the city cemetery on West Third Street, now know as John Paul Park. (She was later moved to the new family plot at Springdale Cemetery.) It is said that souls that are moved from their original burial place don't rest in peace as they should.

Two years later, J.F.D. Lanier remarried, this time a young woman from Pennsylvania named Mary Margaret McClure. James took her to New York City, where he became one of the most successful financiers in his time. They were both later buried in Brooklyn, New York.

After James and Mary moved to New York, eldest son Alexander stayed in the mansion and became its caretaker until James deeded it to him in 1861.

Alex graduated from Yale University. He was very interested in horticulture and managed the grounds, molding them into his vision of a formal garden worthy of the Lanier manor. Through the years, he spent his time involved with civic duties and charitable causes in Madison. After a tornado caused some damage to the house in 1860, he changed the roofline to the then popular mansard style. Alex experienced early heartbreak when Stella Good, the young woman he loved, married another suitor. He remained friends with the couple, and when the husband died, Alex finally married his longtime love. They remained married for the rest of their lives until Stella's death, in the house.

Most volunteers are thrilled to learn and share the Lanier family and house history, even though they have heard the stories about the one that haunts the site. For many years, she has been sighted on the second and third floors. At first, they think she is supposed to be there as part of the atmosphere, dressed for her part in the house museum. But then the realization sets in that she is not a living person. She appears at the end of a hall for a moment or two, or she is seen floating down the mansion's famous cantilevered spiral staircase. The sightings are frequent, and some volunteers leave and won't

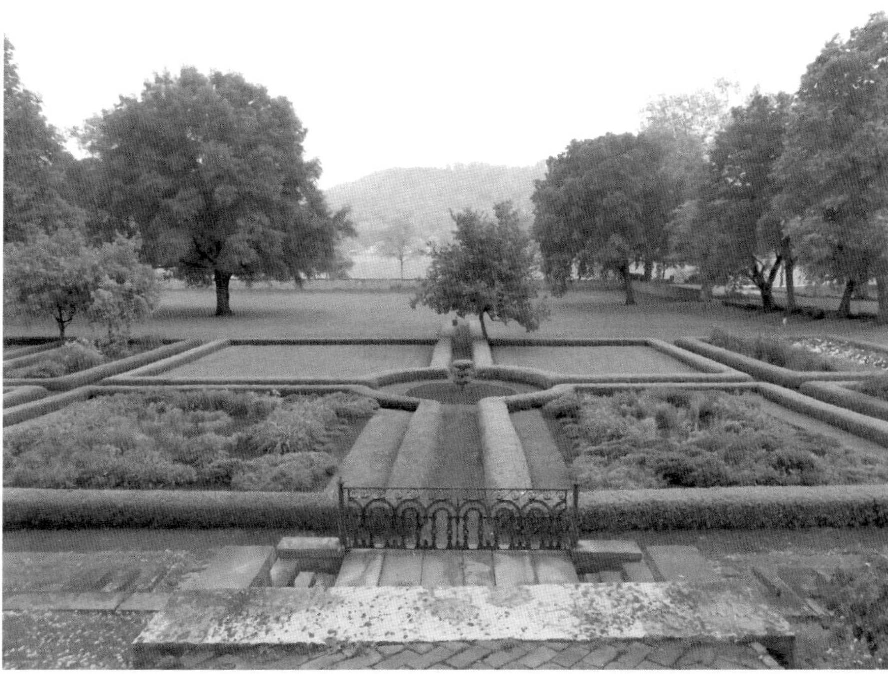

Alexander Lanier was devoted to tending the grounds of the Lanier Mansion.

come back. Even those who don't see her can feel her presence. During preparations for the annual Christmas Candlelight House Tour, a docent was putting decorations around the mirror on the main floor foyer. As she looked into the mirror, she could see in the reflection the lady dressed in red as she passed behind her in front of the beautiful curved door. When she turned around, she was not there.

She doesn't seem to see you but instead just goes about her business, concentrating intently on the moment's task. Some have supposed that she may be one of the former servants. Most believe that she is Mr. Lanier's first wife, Elizabeth, who died in the house, and that seems the most likely. She doesn't seem as though she is in any hurry to move on from the place where she experienced the greatest happiness and the most tragic sadness.

THE PARK AVENUE POLTERGEIST

Nothing fortifies skepticism more than that there are some who are not skeptics; if all were so, they would be wrong.
—Pascal

1001 Park Avenue

Dirk owns his own business as a heating, venting and air conditioning expert. His days are long and demanding, working in all sorts of conditions. For him, when it is cold, it is very cold, and when it is hot, it is sweltering. On this day, he returned home and settled down to get his rest in anticipation of the next day's endeavors. Sleep comes quickly when you work hard, and this evening was no different. But this night would be like no other in his life. He was about to experience something that he would never forget.

As you reach the end of East Main Street, the road changes names not once but twice, in quick succession. First, it changes to Sering Street for the length of a few houses, then at East Second Street, the name changes to Park Avenue/SR-56 as you travel the road out of town. It is confusing to visitors and new residents, but early developers wanted their name attached to the lands that they owned, and after two centuries, they are a part of history. The very first house on the left side is a handsome, two-story, Federal-style brick home. It is another one of those amazing architectural finds in Madison that was not wiped out through so-called progress. You are now in the area of the town of Fulton. Some who live there still call it by that name, but most think it is just a part of Madison, unaware that its strategic position near the Ohio River was the reason for it being settled very early in the area's history. Farmers worked the land here, and a tanner owned a business in the area. Several brewers produced their popular products here.

The area was platted in 1835, and in 1884, the house on Lot 18 was sold to the Gregor Heilman family, who had emigrated from Germany. The Heilmans had three sons and a daughter, all of whom lived in the house. Gregor passed away only three years later in 1887. Much of their family lived in Fulton, and in 1892, his widow, Margarite, brought part of their extended family in to live with them for a short time. The family was close, and members often helped one another out in times of need.

Henry and Daisy Kriel, who were newlyweds and expecting their first child, moved in with their relatives, the Heilmans. Sadly, their baby daughter, Mary (named after Henry's grandmother), arrived stillborn on August 7, 1892. The overwhelming sadness of such a loss is a powerful emotion, one forceful enough to cause an imprint of energy to be made on the location. What adds even further to the terrible sadness is that Daisy died only three years later. We don't know her cause of death, but we can believe that her first child's death had a devastating impact on her.

In the early 1900s, a gas station was erected at 1004 Park Avenue, across the street from the house. It also served as a school and later as a double-sided residence. One of the early residents of that house laughed as she noted that when she was a child, she would go over and drink water out of the big cement trough. She said that it was the coldest water around. She drank there until she found out that it was a horse trough!

Today, the brick building at 1004 Park Avenue is in use as a church. Before the days when it was one of the area's schoolhouses, the surrounding land was utilized as a cemetery until it was repurposed. Those buried there were moved to the new city cemetery on Third Street (now John Paul Park).

It is not known if all the bodies in the first cemetery were ever moved to Third Street or if they were washed away in the seasonal floodwaters. It appears that some were moved more than once, with the relocation of the city cemetery once again in 1859, from Third Street to Springdale Cemetery.

The home remained in the possession of various Heilman family members for ninety-two years until it was purchased by Dirk's family in

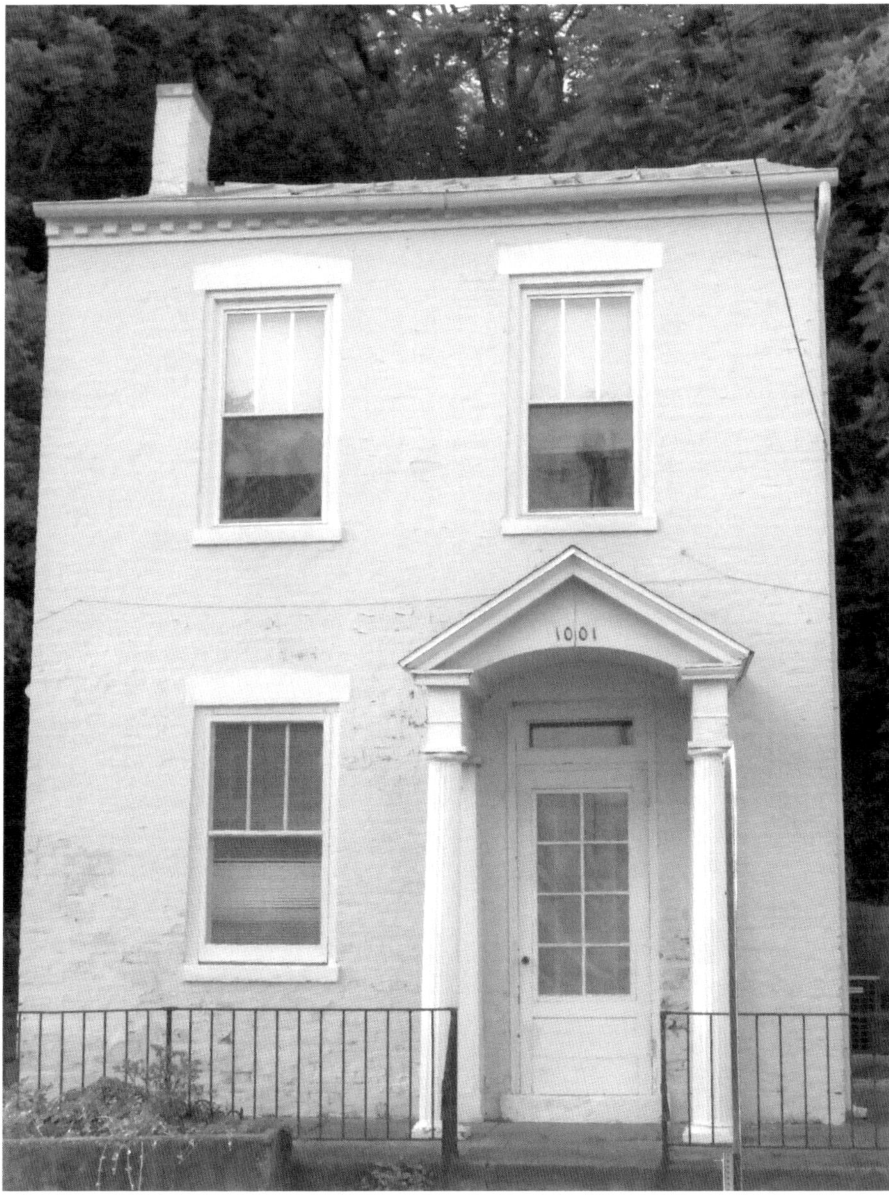

The former home of the young woman who returns to look for her lost baby, Mary, who died the day she was born.

1976. But it seems that some of the long-departed family members still visit. On that particular night, as Dirk slept deeply, a sliver of moonlight coming through the window split the darkness of the room. His even breathing was suddenly broken as he was stirred from the depths of his sleep. Something had compelled him to open his eyes. It was that feeling you get when you realize that you are not alone in a room. As he looked around, he saw something that would have alarmed anyone. Standing in the doorway was a young woman, with long flowing hair. She had a transparent appearance and was dressed in an "old-fashioned white gown." As she stood there, Dirk stayed very still, not certain what to do. They stared at each other. She seemed to be comfortable in the room, but what gave him a sense of panic was that she was staring right at him, with her eyes locked on his. She said nothing but seemed to want to tell him something. Finally, after what seemed like ten minutes of staring at each other, he asked if he could help her. That seemed to break the spell, and she slowly began to disappear, starting at her feet and moving upward to her head until she was not there anymore. He said it was as if a wind blew her out of the room. Her disappearance left a void in the room for a moment where she had stood seconds before.

For a little while, Dirk sat looking at the spot where the invasive visitor had been. His mind began to review what had just happened. When he finally got his nerves to calm down and his mind to settle, he went back to sleep just before dawn to try to get a bit of sleep before having to get up and start his workday. Although another person experiencing this startling encounter might be afraid to go back into the room—or the building, for that matter—Dirk said that he was not afraid. He felt very peaceful about the visitation, as though she just wanted someone to help her in some way.

Had it been Daisy, the young woman who had lost her first child while living in the house? Had she returned to look for her lost babe? Does the overwhelming sadness of losing her infant keep her spirit forever tied to the house? Or had one of the restless spirits risen from her forgotten tomb across the street, trying to let someone know that she was still there?

Dirk wondered if he should share his experience with anyone. He ended up keeping the story to himself for several weeks, even though he knows others who have had experiences in this house and in other houses in town. That is the way with these phenomena. People don't want to be thought of as irrational, even though so many in town have had experiences themselves or know someone who has. He said that others who have lived in the house since then have moved out because they realized that it's haunted and were too afraid to stay there. The current resident has lived there for the last four years. She knows of its background and has heard walking on the floor above when no one is there, as well as other strange sounds, but she doesn't feel threatened. A person's reaction to the affected buildings reflects their view of the spirit world. Some are very accepting, but others are very fearful. Still others don't even want to admit that it is going on. But these visitations do happen. And they happen very frequently in Madison.

The Ohio Theater Fright Show

The day Science begins to study non-physical phenomena, it will make more progress in one decade than in all the previous centuries of its existence.
—Nikola Tesla

105 East Main Street

It is well known in the paranormal field that every theater has a ghost or two. Theaters all over the world have had reports of paranormal activity because it is thought that theaters are settings that inspire and stir strong emotions. The energy of emotions is thought to become imprinted on the environment. And if you think about it, various places do feel different accordingly. Usually funeral homes feel solemn and heavy, churches feel light and uplifting, historic sites feel potent with power, homes feel warm and welcoming and workplaces feel sterile and hard. Our surroundings affect our feelings. One of my favorite sayings is by Winston Churchill, who said, "We shape our dwellings and afterwards our dwellings shape us."

Theaters are like repositories of emotions. When you think about the full range of emotions felt during a movie or play, you can understand the lingering energy left in the environment. Sadness, horror, joy, amusement, edginess, anticipation, heartbreak and hilarity—all strong feelings that you can almost grasp in their intensity when you are surrounded in a room by people expressing them.

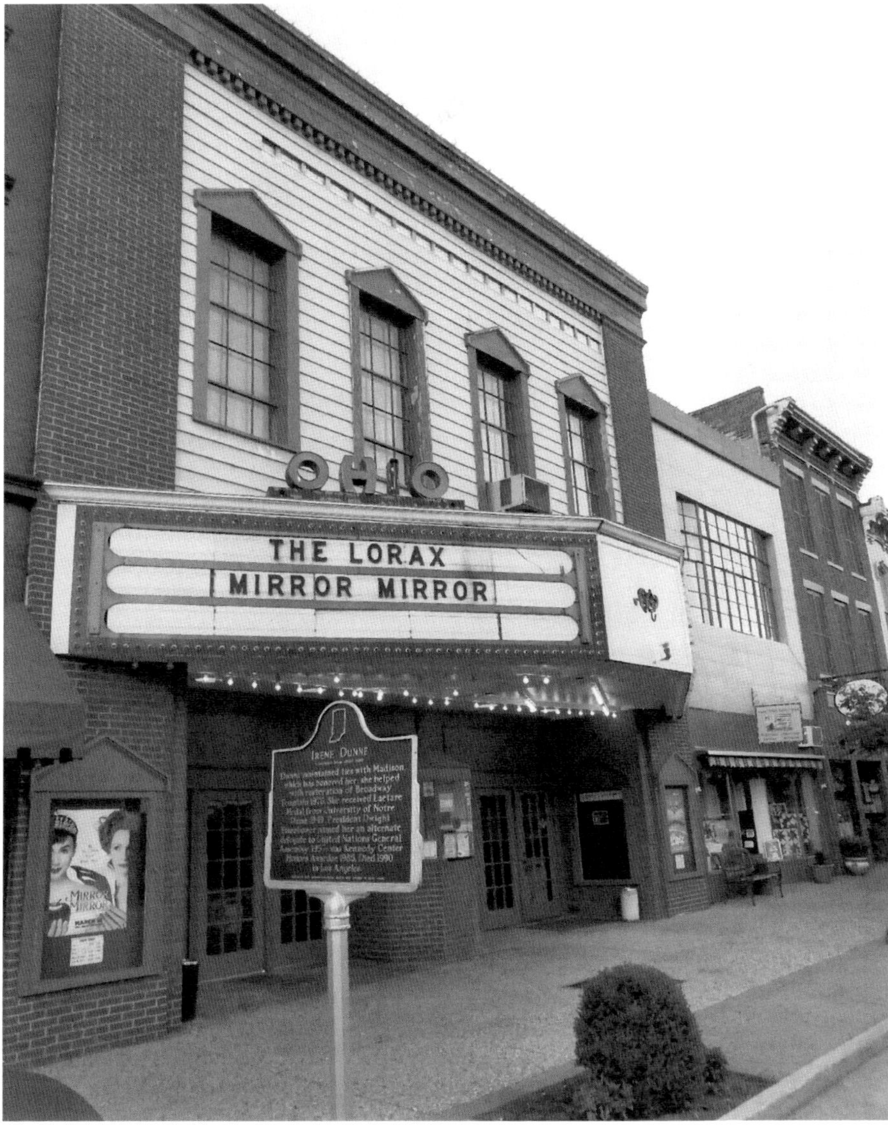

The Ohio Theater, a wonderful old-fashioned movie theater with its own spectral customers.

The Ohio Theater sits in the middle of the main commercial district on Main Street. The site had operated as a nickelodeon in the early part of the twentieth century until it was converted into a movie theater. A Kilgen organ was installed in the theater in 1928 to lend ambiance to the silent movies, but by the 1940s, it had been moved to a local school. It has since been sold into private hands.

The first theater, called the Little Grand Theater, burned down in 1937 but was rebuilt in 1938. The name was changed a few more times, to the Madison and then to the Ohio Theater. Today, it's a double theater that plays mid-run family films and hosts the occasional play or live event.

Elizabeth Buchanan has worked at the theater for nine years. During that time, she has heard a number of stories and has had her own experience or two. When she first started working there, she was told by other employees that years earlier, a man had hanged himself on the balcony. That seems to be where most of the unsettling activity takes place. While working, patrons have come up to tell her that they have seen people sitting up in the corner of the balcony who disappear while they are looking right at them. She said that one of her encounters took place on the same empty balcony when she was cleaning; she heard what sounded like someone snapping their fingers right next to her ear.

The bathrooms are a long trip down a dark stairway to the basement, and patrons have said that they feel like they are not alone as they make their way there and that they hear voices in the room when they are there alone.

One evening, a former employee was working in the office that opens up to the balcony when she saw a young boy with blond hair run across the aisle in front of the door. The theater was empty except for her, and seeing the apparition that she knew was not a living person scared her so much that she ran out of the theater. She called the owners from another location and told them that she was not coming back. A high school student who worked on weekends said that he didn't like sweeping up on the balcony because he was "creeped out" and had seen dark black shadows move up there among the seats.

The theater's reputation has spread as a hotbed of activity, and many paranormal groups ask to come and explore the location from the basement to the upper levels. When I spoke to Elizabeth, she said that a regional group had just done an investigation a few weeks before.

Visiting an old-fashioned movie theater is a rare opportunity that is quickly disappearing with the last of the small theaters being replaced with newer multiplex versions. People who have attended events or viewed movies at the Ohio say that "you can't beat the atmosphere and that it is an experience that everyone should have before they are all gone." But realize when you visit that you might just have more memories to take away with you than you had planned on.

The Little Girl Ghost of Walnut Street

Now it is the time of night
That the graves, all gaping wide,
Every one lets forth his sprite
In the church-way paths to glide.
—William Shakespeare

712–714 Walnut Street

She was standing at the counter chopping vegetables for her family's dinner when she heard the click. She grimaced as she scooped the potatoes in her hands and dropped them into the casserole dish. She knew what it was. Looking up, the light of the television got brighter as it came on. It was just a little irritation, but it was happening more and more frequently. She stopped to listen and heard voices talking loudly upstairs. Shaking her head, she realized that the TV had turned on up there, too. She went on finishing her tasks, irritated by the incident as if it was a minor inconvenience and unafraid but just getting tired of the pestering. That was how she described the outbreak of baffling events.

Corinna has a friendly, open, upbeat personality and didn't show the least bit of hesitation about telling the story of her poltergeist experiences. She and her family have lived in the house for six years now and seem very happy in their cozy three-bedroom home. She says it was built in 1865 but is sure that it sits where another house existed before. In the area that was

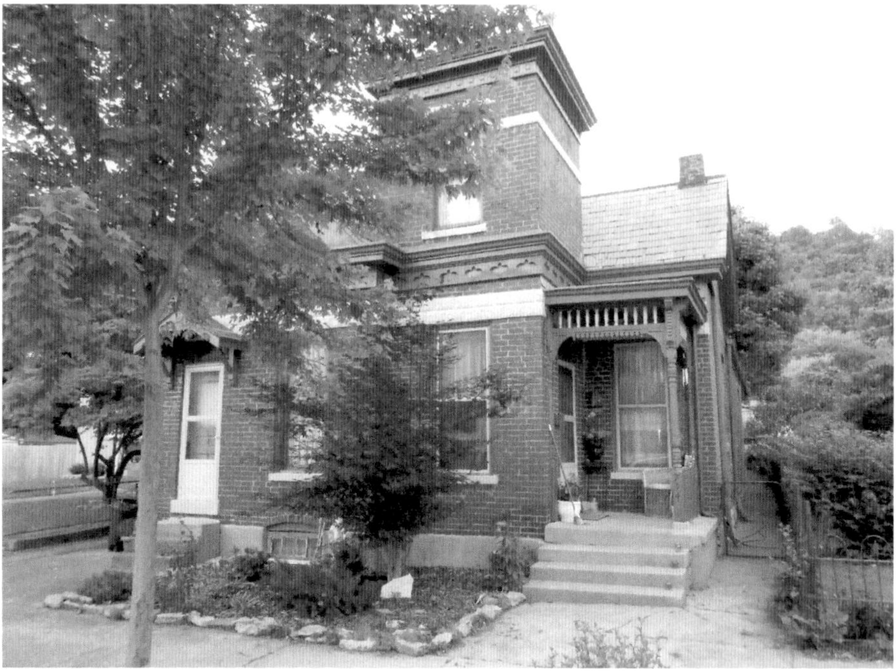

An enchanting Italianate home where young girls who come to live in the house like to play with a little ghost in the bedroom on the north-side corner of the house.

once known as Georgetown, most of the surrounding houses were built in the 1830s. She went on to tell me about how she came to live in the house where her family has had many unusual experiences.

She was a "military brat" who traveled throughout her childhood. After living in Oregon for twenty-six years, she decided that she would love to give her children the comforting lifestyle of a small midwestern river town and chose Madison, Indiana. When looking for a house for herself, husband Ted and two daughters Nakia and Abby, Corinna knew that she would recognize the perfect home when she saw it. After looking at several houses with her realtor, they parked outside this brick Italianate home, and she instantly loved its look. It is a whimsical and detailed example of the style, with charming, exaggerated ornamentation. It reminded her of the historic buildings found out west, and she couldn't wait to look inside. Walking through the door convinced her that she had found the right house. Her realtor said, "Are we finished looking?" Corinna confirmed that they were.

Upon returning to Oregon to move her family, the excitement about the impending adventure influenced their good friends Jill and her partner Hoppy to move as well. While visiting Corinna's new home and taking photos in the rooms, Jill cautiously made it known that she believed that her friend's new residence was haunted. She must be one of the intuitive people who possess that extra sense. Corinna and her family moved into the house anyway. A little while later, Jill presented evidence to prove her point. The photographs she took showed floating globes that were not seen in the room when they were taken. Corinna and family had already realized that there was something going on in their house. Jill and Hoppy decided that maybe Madison wasn't for them and moved back to Oregon.

Corinna and family had only lived in the house for a very short time before they began to experience what seemed to be the tricks of a very mischievous spirit. Although they were often surprised by the activity of the unseen prankster, they were becoming accustomed to the unusual episodes that occurred "like clockwork" in their home. As much as they tried to attribute logical reasons for the incidents, they very quickly came to grips with the knowledge that the performances were not just flukes or electrical quirks when the other events began to unfold.

By now, both husband and wife had both seen the "glowing balls." One night, when making a parental check on Abby, their youngest daughter, Corinna noticed that glowing spheres were dancing around the room, not seeming to care that an audience was spellbound by the display. She called to her husband to bear witness to the incredible spectacle. They remembered the photographs that Jill had taken, and now this visual manifestation reinforced the proof.

Over the next several months, the rascally sprite continued to play pranks on the family. The couple would arrive home from work to find that their little white poodle-maltese Tiki was not in the kennel where he had been left that morning. A quick search of the house would find him confined in the bathroom with the door closed. A few more of those incidents began to cause a bit of worry. She was concerned about the well-being of her pooch and thought that if the ghost could take their dog out of his cage, what else could it do?

Possessing an inquisitive nature, Corinna knew that the time had come to take a more proactive approach. She needed to find out what or who was causing the disruption in her home. So, one day, she planned a day off work and, along with youngest daughter Abby, initiated a "house history day." It presented a great opportunity to spend a day with her daughter and teach a few lessons about knowing your town's history and how you fit into its story.

The two investigators started out at city hall, going through archival records and successfully finding the names of the former owners, as well as taking away a copy of the original deed. They made a memorable day of the outing, stopping for a tasty lunch at one of the charming restaurants in the historic downtown. After their lunch, the pair headed on to the Jefferson County Historical Society Research Center, where they found photographs of the house in earlier times. Some of the photos showed men outside the building next door, wearing aprons and surrounded by saddletrees. A saddletree is the wooden foundation of a saddle that is covered by leather.

After leaving the research center, a trip to the local library netted some additional nuggets of information. They found out that the original owner was a man named August Schmidt, a saddletree maker from Prussia, and his wife, Katarina. He owned the saddletree factory located by the house on the next lot. Census records revealed that Mr. and Mrs. Schmidt had two children, a son and a daughter named Susan. They lived in the house for five years. Corinna also found by viewing old newspapers on microfiche that a wake had been held in her house for a young twenty-two-year-old man named Mathias who had died in Missouri. She thought that perhaps he was a relative of the family and that this energy had brought about some of the paranormal activity. Further research turned up information that the house was owned by single women from the 1880s to the 1930s.

Finding and assembling all the information had filled in a lot of blanks. Because of the mischievous, childlike pranks, Corinna had always suspected that the spirit haunting their home was a child. After their day of historic investigation, they believed that they had found the answer to their question of who was haunting their home.

The title search turned up another interesting piece of information. Abby was in junior high at the time, and the school's science teacher was listed as a previous owner of their house. Her mother said to tell the teacher that they lived in the house now. Abby was excited to tell the teacher the interesting news, but when she did, the teacher became pale, her face froze and her eyes widened. She said, "You live in *that* house?" Apparently, she didn't have fond memories of her time living there. Later, Corinna had an opportunity to ask her more in-depth questions about the experiences that she had. The teacher said that things would move around and that they also had trouble with electrical items. She would put an item down and then would not be able to find it. Later, it would show up in a different room. Corinna's family had been having the very same issues. She had never seen anything, but her daughter would often ask if her mother saw "the old woman standing in the room with them." The teacher also said that her daughter would talk and play with the little girl ghost in her bedroom on the north side of the house—the same bedroom that Abby now occupied and the room where Corinna would often find her own daughter playing with an unseen friend.

I was amused and impressed by Corinna's reaction to the haunting of her house. She spoke about it as though an unruly relative had showed up unexpectedly and just moved on in. It exposed her adaptive personality of dealing with the situation that she was given.

Later, a psychic visited the house, but Corinna said that she didn't tell her any of the background information that she had found so it wouldn't corrupt any information that may be revealed. According to the psychic, the original owner had a daughter (she "felt" her name was Susan) who had died at a young age, perhaps about five years old, in the house. She said that the little girl had likely died from exhaustion from being overworked at the saddletree factory. In those days, there were no child labor laws, and all family members contributed their part to the family business. Corinna was skeptical about the cause that the psychic attributed to Susan's death but never about her presence. It does seem strange that a family would let their five-year-old daughter become overworked to the point of death.

There were many times when Abby would come into her parents' bedroom in the middle of the night, upset that the TV had turned on by itself and was playing so loudly that it had woken her up. It seems that the little specter wanted attention, but it was causing problems with sleep loss and uncertainty about the safety of the pets. So, with some angst and sadness over making such a dramatic decision, they decided that the time had come to stop the visitations.

Corinna learned from the psychic that the way to send a spirit "into the light" was to perform a ritual by burning sage leaves and saying prayers throughout the house. After putting up with all the attention-grabbing shenanigans of the little girl ghost for so long, the family carried out the ritual to release her spirit. Afterward, the house seemed to become very quiet and empty. They are pretty certain that she's gone, but they feel a little sad because she had been a part of their lives for three years. Ted misses her. After all, she didn't mean any harm. She just wanted to play with the family sharing her home. Her premature death separated her from her own family. I expect that she is happy to be reunited with them. That doesn't mean she won't be back to visit.

Judge Jeremiah Sullivan's House

Be silent in that solitude,
Which is not loneliness—for then
The spirits of the dead, who stood
In life before thee, are again
In death around thee, and their will
Shall overshadow thee; be still.
—Edgar Allan Poe

209 West Second Street

It is known not only as the first mansion in Madison but also as the first mansion in the Northwest Territory. The red brick Federal house was built in the early 1820s outside what were then the existing city boundaries. Jeremiah Sullivan was a lawyer who had come to the western frontier from Virginia. He had served in the War of 1812 and attended the College of William and Mary. He came to the town, purchased some land and built his beautiful house. He was involved in much of the shaping of early Indiana. It is said that he suggested the name of the new capital, "Indianapolis." He was very influential in the early days of Indiana, serving as a state legislator and an Indiana Supreme Court justice, and he helped found Hanover College and the Indiana Historical Society.

Sullivan and his wife, Charlotte, had twelve children. The eight older children all lived to adulthood, except for Frances, who died at fifteen.

Frances, known to all as Fanny, has the distinction of being the first to be buried at Springdale after its official designation as the city cemetery in 1839. It was quite a challenge to raise a child to adulthood during the nineteenth century. Infections, epidemics, accidents and a lack of medicines to treat common illnesses all contributed to the loss of so many children. Of the last four Sullivan children, three died in infancy, with the fourth, little Julia, living to the age of six.

The oldest son, Thomas, served as a captain during the Mexican-American War. The Civil War split the family, like so many others, with son Algernon aligning his allegiance as a Southern sympathizer and Jeremiah Jr. attending the Naval Academy in Annapolis and serving as a Union general. Sullivan was most proud of Jerry Jr., for his son's political stance reflected his own. Even though he had performed gallantly on the field through many campaigns, his superior officer blamed him for the loss of ground, and his career was stalled. Disillusioned by what seemed to be an unfair accusation, he ended up moving to California after the war, and even though he was trained as a lawyer, he spent the rest of his life in various clerical positions.

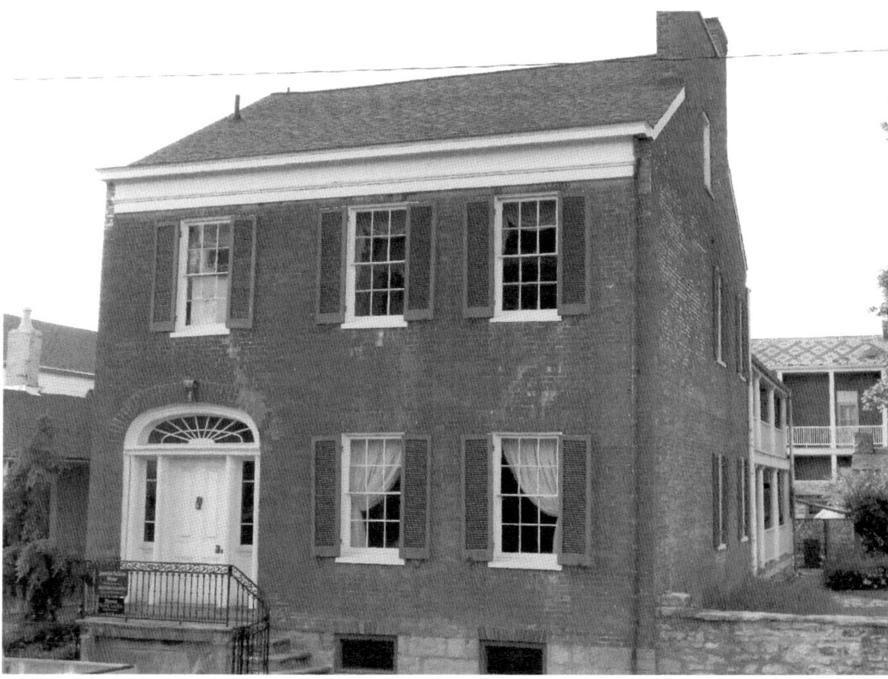

Judge Jeremiah Sullivan's beautiful Federal-style house on Second Street. Today, it is owned by Historic Madison Inc. and is open to the public.

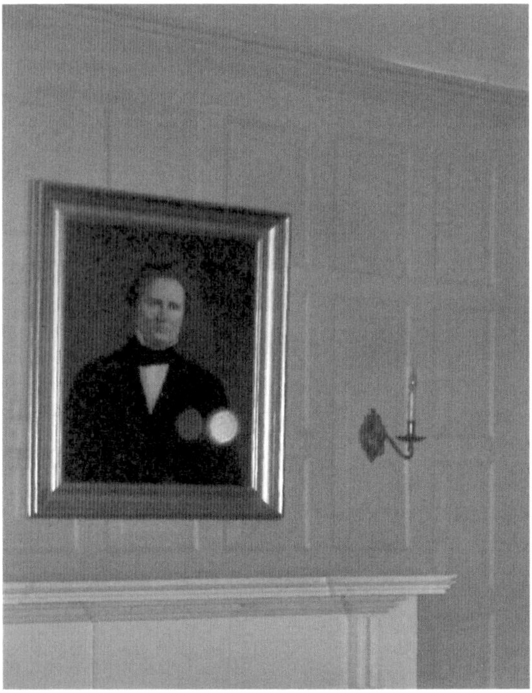

Left: Close-up of the orb in front of the portrait. It is reflected in the oil painting.

Below: Upstairs bedroom in the Sullivan House. Notice the orb hovering near the portrait.

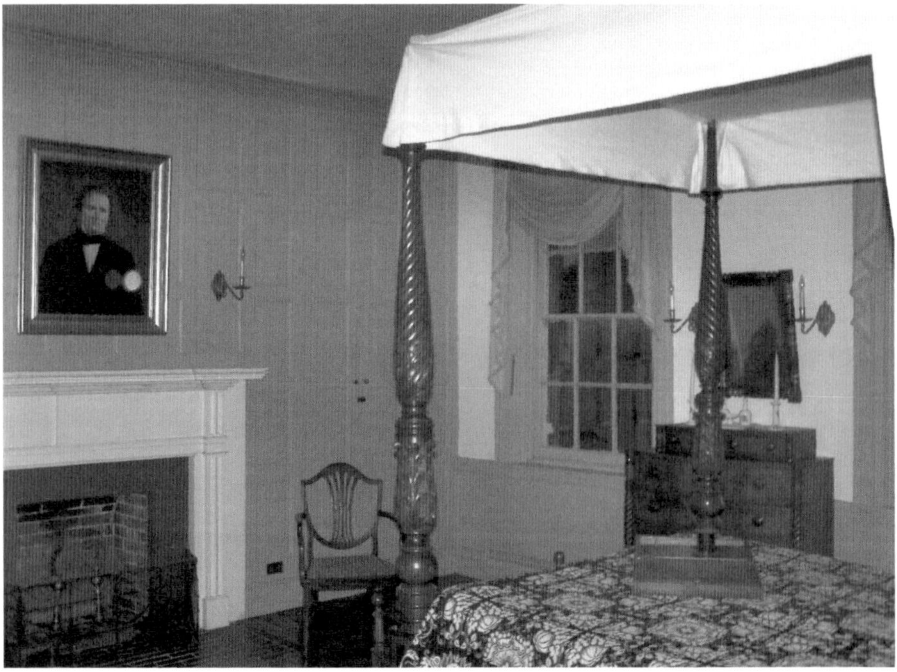

Son Algernon, along with partner William Cromwell, was the founder of a law firm in New York that survives to this day, and it is known as one of the most prestigious law firms in the world. His Southern loyalties led him to defend the crew of the *Savannah*, the first Confederate ship captured and put on trial in the North. Algernon was arrested as a traitor and incarcerated at Fort Lafayette prison in New York City. His health was also affected by the experience. He was there for six weeks and then released. One day later, Abraham Lincon's secretary of state, William H. Seward sent word *not* to release him because there was new evidence. But the New York City police did not arrest him. He was thought to possess every high moral characteristic and was well loved and admired by those who knew and worked with him. By 1875, his reputation in New York had recovered to the point that many wanted him to run for mayor, but he declined.

Today, the Sullivan House is owned by Historic Madison Inc. and is open for public tours. When I came to visit the house, it was as a part of a private tour for the local Jefferson County Civil War Roundtable. Jan Vetrhus led the guided tour in the first person as Jeremiah's wife, Charlotte Sullivan. As she led the party through the house, I lagged behind at the back of the group to take photos, hoping as always to capture evidence of a haunt. Sure enough, in one of the upper bedrooms, in front of the portrait of a middle-aged Judge Sullivan, an orb was captured hovering. Not only was it floating in the air, but it was also reflected in the oil painting, providing evidence that it was not just a reflection of a flash but something that was in front of the painting rather than on it. Orbs are very difficult to see with the naked eye, although they have been seen. But they are caught very frequently by digital cameras in phantom-laden areas, often in different colors. Is this Judge Sullivan still roaming the home where he lived when he secured his place in Indiana history? Or is it one of the children who passed away in the house, comforted by the familiar likeness of their father?

The Murder of Sheriff Robert Right Rea

For who can wonder that man should feel a vague belief in tales of disembodied spirits wandering through those places which they once dearly affected, when he himself, scarcely less separated from his old world than they, is forever lingering upon past emotions and bygone times, and hovering, the ghost of his former self, about the places and people that warmed his heart of old?
—Charles Dickens

507–509 Walnut Street
318 East Main Street

During the early1850s, Jefferson County and the area surrounding Madison, Indiana, experienced an economic boom. Madison's position directly across from Kentucky, on the Ohio River, offered a great advantage as the river brought settlers, trade and prosperity. In 1850, Madison was the largest town in Indiana. Row houses along with Federal- and Greek Revival–style homes were being built as the town expanded. The wealthy were trying their best to outdo one another by building the grandest homes in the region.

Several blocks away, in the section known as Georgetown, free blacks had settled with their families, hoping to build a new life and prosper in the state of Indiana. The census from 1820 recorded 48 black families living in Madison, and by 1850, there were 298 black families. Today, Georgetown's significance is remembered with a historical marker at Fifth and Jefferson Streets. Many of the original buildings still stand.

The Fugitive Slave Act, which noted that runaway slaves must be returned to their "owners," was enacted in 1850. Madison's proximity to the slave state of Kentucky allowed for stealthy escapes across the Ohio River to find refuge in the town. During many years in the summer and fall, the river was so shallow at points that one could walk across it. During some winters, the river would freeze solid, also making crossing viable. Several abolitionists lived and worked in the area, assisting those who escaped the bonds of slavery yet breaking the laws of that time.

In this setting, Robert Right Rea served as the Jefferson County sheriff. He came to Madison as a sixteen-year-old and did quite well for himself. He married, had eight children and worshiped at the Presbyterian church. Rea was also a farmer and a successful businessman who at a certain point owned two hotels and a few stables. He had owned one of the stables in Georgetown since at least 1837. The Federal-style brick building is still standing today at 507–511 Walnut Street.

Dennis Jorgensen, who portrayed Sheriff Rea for the Madison Bicentennial in 2009, speculated that the sheriff used his stables there to observe the

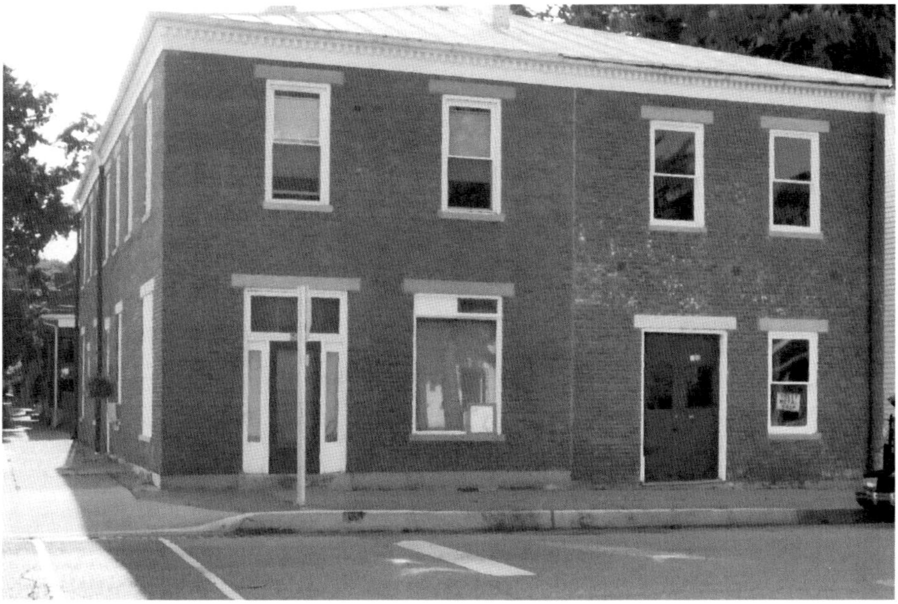

Sheriff Robert Right Rea's stable on Walnut Street, in Georgetown, as it looks today.

comings and goings of area residents—that way he would know who belonged there, and who was new in the area. There have been legendary accounts that say that one of the best-known abolitionists, "George De Baptiste, would 'borrow' horses from Sheriff Rea's stable to usher runaways out of the area and place the horses back in the barn by morning. Later in his life, he said in an interview, that he often shod the horse's shoes with carpet to muffle the noise."

Sheriff Rea was reported to be a well-built man of ordinary size who had a reputation for being a kind man in spite of his chosen profession. He was said to be "very proficient at performing his duties of chasing down horse thieves, murders and runaway slaves," all the lawbreakers of the time. The two characteristics may seem at odds, but the morals of that time are impossible to reconcile when looking at the past through modern eyes. He took over as sheriff for William Wharton, who resigned while in office in the early 1850s, but lost his bid to be elected in 1854. He went about tending his businesses until at the age of sixty-nine, when he became a part of a murder mystery that remains an unsolved cold case to this day.

The following is the actual report in the *Daily Courier* on Tuesday May, 11, 1869. Such graphic descriptions would never be seen in today's news reports. It would certainly require a warning about the content, if it was.

> *The body found at Mann's Landing, below Hanover, yesterday, proved to be that of R.R. Rea. It was identified by several persons beyond a peradventure. Mr. Rea disappeared on the 8th of March last, over two months ago, and notwithstanding all the efforts made at the time, no clue could be found to his disappearance until yesterday. It was suspected at the time that he had been foully dealt with, but everybody was loath to believe that any one could bear malice against "Uncle Right" sufficient to imbrue his hands with murder; but the marks on the old man's head prove the suspicions to have been only too true. The skull on both sides of his head was found to be broken in with some instrument alike the leaden ball on the head of a rattan cane. But most likely the murderous instrument used by the perpetrator was a slugshot. When found, every particle of clothing was off the body with the exception of one sock. The body was very natural and not discolored in the least, showing that it could not long have been exposed to the air, and no other part of the body showed signs of violence. How his clothing got off his body is an unexplained mystery, unless they were taken off by the miscreant who committed the murder to prevent the identification of the body in case it was ever caught, and thereby conceal the murderer.*

The last seen of "Uncle Right" was about 9 o'clock on Monday night, March 8th, in company with an entire stranger, to all who seen them pass out of the house, with whom he had been talking about going up into Switzerland county to buy hogs. We cannot but think that he was murdered for the money he was supposed to possess, as no one who knew him could have been so hard hearted as to send his own soul to eternal perdition, by murdering him for any petty or imaginary wrong.

His body was decently incased in a coffin and brought up to the city yesterday evening, and deposited in the vault at Springdale Cemetery to await the arrival of his son R.R. Rea Jr., who is on board the steamer Richmond, and has been telegraphed for.

He was buried at Underwood Cemetery, where many of his relations lie, on the hilltop in Madison.

This incident is not an unusual occurrence for that time. Unscrupulous thugs perpetrated similar swindles throughout the country. The story of another such crime that took place locally was retold in the book *Murder in the House of God* by Dave Taylor. In 1878, John Beavers, was caught after the murder of John Sewell, an elderly man, whom he had lured out into the countryside, supposedly to purchase land. He planned the murder to seize the money that the victim would be carrying to complete the transaction. After being led in and out of the county for several days, the opportunity to do the deed finally presented itself to the miscreant. While the elderly gentleman was taking a much-needed rest in a church, Beavers bashed in the old man's head. He proceeded to set the church on fire, a strategic mistake, because it alerted neighbors, bringing them running to put out the fire. They found the bloody, beaten body while attempting to subdue the flames. Fortunately, the criminal was caught before getting away, unlike the murderer of Sheriff Rea. John Beavers told a friend that he "had conceived the idea about one year ago, as I and another partner were talking about making a 'raise.' The other party had killed three men."

John Beavers was caught for the murder of Mr. Sewell, which took place nine years after the murder of Robert Right Rea. Could the "other party" be the one responsible for the unsolved murder of Sheriff Rea? It may or may not have been, but the disclosure demonstrates that there were devious persons in the area who could hatch a plan to lure a man away to murder him for the money he carried. Those elderly persons who had some means seemed to have been targeted and were especially vulnerable.

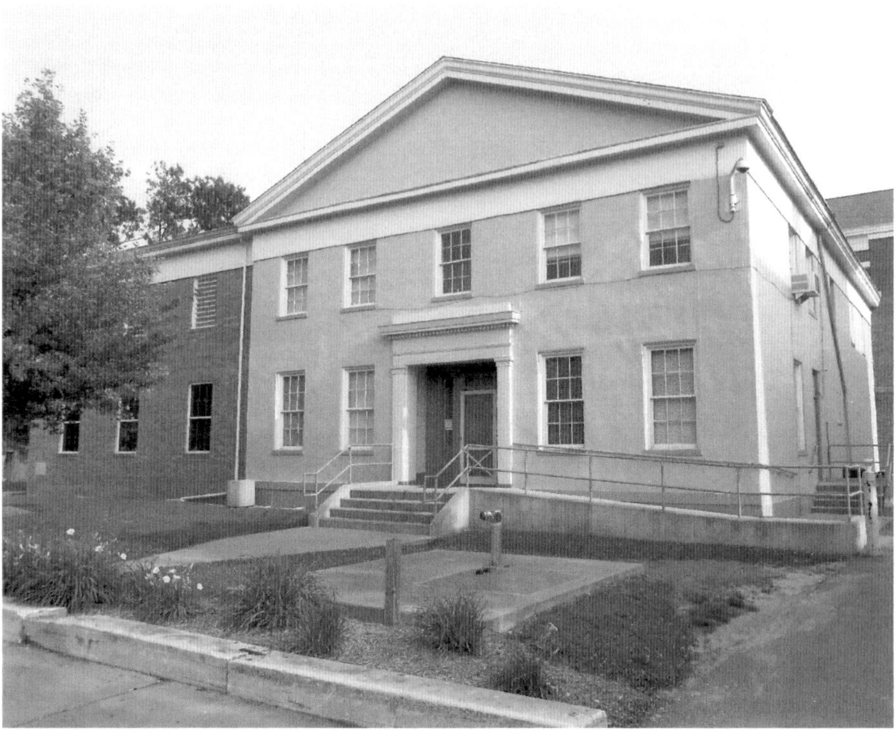

The Old City Jail, built when R.R. Rea was sheriff in 1849–50. Its walls are two feet thick, and people who have been incarcerated here report that they are not alone in the cell.

Beavers was hanged in the courthouse and jail yard, with people coming from miles around to see the only court-ordered hanging in Jefferson County. Some brought picnic baskets as they stood on rooftops and gathered around to watch.

The Old County Jail was built in 1849–50 and is one of the rare nineteenth-century jailhouse buildings still standing in Indiana. Its walls are two feet thick, built of native limestone from Marble Hill Quarry in Saluda. It was built during the time when Rea was sheriff. Walking through the inside, it looks much like an old castle dungeon. The key used to open the huge door lock is hefty and a foot in length. The jail is still in use today, mostly as storage. During the 1970s, those incarcerated often yelled out in fright that they were not alone in the cells. People like to visit, but many who tour the old jail describe it using terms like "haunted," "possessed" and "eerie."

Today, neighbors who live by the old stable on Walnut Street report sounds at night like horse's hooves clomping down a brick street in front of the former stable building. The jingling sound of harnesses is heard approaching, getting louder and then fading again. Could the former abolitionists still be acting out their nightly adventures in a ghostly form? Sheriff Rea was proud of the new jailhouse, too. He spent time there as sheriff during the first four years of its existence, locking up regional lawbreakers. The unsolved and violent end to Sheriff Rea certainly qualifies his former properties as likely locations for paranormal activity.

THE HILLTOP HORROR

Houses are not haunted. We *are haunted, and regardless of the architecture with which we surround ourselves, our ghosts stay with us until we ourselves are ghosts.*
—*Dean Koontz*

Clifty Drive, one-fourth mile west of the Clifty Falls State Park entrance

Some people become visibly frightened when talking about the unknown. I have seen people who become so anxious that they get up and walk around during a conversation involving ghost stories. What makes them so nervous? What are they afraid of? Not knowing what the spirits have in mind is frightening when you realize that you have no control over what they do.

People may live in a house for years and never have any kind of supernatural experiences in the building. Yet if a different person moves in, all types of events may occur. What triggers the events is unknown. Perhaps that person is a relative or just someone the entity wants to be around. In some cases, the dead can become so powerful that they need to be exorcised. No one needs that kind of negative energy around.

Some people are sensitive to changes in atmosphere or environment and are able to invoke an ability called psychokinesis, or the ability to move objects and cause unexplained occurrences. Like those with psychic abilities, this trait can be hereditary and may be triggered by severe emotional distress.

The haunting of Madison is not confined to just the historic district, although naturally that is where most reports arise. In 1995, a book was written about a house on the hilltop that was so possessed that it drove out all its tenants in a short span of time, just after they moved in. That is, until one family who had invested all their sweat and money in the property stayed to fight off the many attacks by paranormal demons. At one time, the property had cabins used by visitors and a popular restaurant. Employees began to describe strange happenings. Floating lights, moving items, breaking glass, popping light bulbs and other bizarre occurrences were reported.

In her book *The People in the Attic*, one woman described every type of possession and haunting, so sinister that one could find similar events depicted in the most frightening horror movie. Her house, a ranch-style mid-century example made of Bedford stone, is located on Clifty Drive. It had been the site of abuse and murder in the past, and the energy that was created caused so much terror and pain for this family that I don't know how they had the strength to fight the depth of the evil that they encountered. The property was once known as the Windrift Hotel and Restaurant before they converted it to their family home. This particular mayhem was exacerbated by the insidious paranormal causes from the surrounding environment and disturbances created from her own psychic abilities.

After seeking assistance from the local Catholic church, demonologists, psychics and mediums, she discovered an extrasensory ability from within, and after learning how to exert some control over it, she finally came to a degree of peace. The house was featured on numerous television shows and news reports in this and other countries. This is an example of one of the rare but extreme disturbances that can occur from supernatural activity when the environment is marked with psychic scars.

The Playful Spirit

What beck'ning ghost along the moonlight shade
Invites my steps, and points to yonder glade?
—Alexander Pope

Some spirits cause what may seem like a disturbance, but in reality they are trying to let us know that they are all right. Ellie Smith, a well-known local artist, told me about an incident that made such an impression on her that she said it was something she would never forget.

It happened soon after her father's funeral. She and some of her family went to her father's house to sort out business and make decisions about the estate. While standing in the kitchen, they began to hear sounds coming from the basement. When the noises didn't stop, they decided to go downstairs and investigate. Her kids nervously made fun of the situation, saying, "Oooh! Scary!"

As the family cautiously crept down the stairs, all sticking close together, they could hear the rhythmic noise getting louder as they got nearer to the basement floor. As their eyes adjusted to the darkness of the room, they walked toward the area from which the sound was coming. It only took a few seconds before they had found the source of the disturbance. There in one of the corners of the basement was a rocking horse, moving back and forth on its own and showing no sign of stopping. It was an old antique rocking horse that her father had purchased years before—one on which her youngest son had often played. Spirits often return to places where they were happy in their lives. She believed that he was letting them know that he was okay and having a good time with an old amusement. Even so, they all ran out of the basement pretty quickly.

THE CITY CEMETERIES OF MADISON

Thy soul shall find itself alone
'Mid dark thoughts of the grey tomb-stone;
Not one, of all the crowd, to pry
Into thine hour of secrecy.
—Edgar Allan Poe, "Spirits of the Dead"

Cemeteries have long been associated with sadness and eerie, uneasy feelings. You picture fog-enveloped gravestones as you listen for signs of movement and rustling leaves alerting you to uninvited and unwelcome visitors. The fear of death, and the corresponding purpose for the land set aside for entombment of our lifeless bodies, brings on feelings of dread and trepidation.

The advent of digital photographs has allowed the capture of all sorts of anomalies believed to be spirit manifestations. Photographs taken in cemeteries often show orbs, strange floating circular objects that appear to have some type of glowing energy inside. They are thought to be the concentrated energy of departed people, now manifesting as spirit balls. The advanced technology has provided the ability to prove the existence of activity that has been reported for centuries, but without the ability to substantiate it with tangible proof. Many mediums say that spirits would not want to linger in a cemetery because of their dependence on energy and the seeming lack of that force in a cemetery. Throughout history, though, there have been reports of visitations and sightings in cemeteries, and now modern photographic and voice detection technologies are confirming that belief.

It seems that the locations that had been chosen for burials early on in the settlement of Madison became inconvenient as more and more immigrants came and the city limits expanded. Meetings were advertised in the local newspaper calling for residents to discuss the method of removal and reburial of the interred. What had seemed at one time like a fine location for the resting place of a loved one later became problematic as the demand for building locations increased. The original property owners may have died without descendants, or the property that they owned may have been sold to someone else. The existence of family plots on land that was now owned by people with no relation to the dearly departed created a problem for the new owners. They would have to maintain the graves of people to whom they had no connection.

Madison city limits are constrained because to the east, the area between the Ohio River and the foothills dwindles to a sliver of land. This makes construction improbable because of the seasonal flooding, and if you build opposite of the river, on the hillside, you would have to climb up a steep hill to get to your front door. Most chose not to build in that direction, and so the corporation lines ended where the narrowing begins.

On the far west end, the land is cut off by foothills that sweep down to the Ohio River itself. Thus the city has a beautiful setting, but expansion beyond the east and west land limits had proven most difficult. Eventually, construction did begin to spread out at the top of the hill, to the north, in what would eventually become the independent city of North Madison. In North Madison, they also had their problems with family plots, being placed in spots that created havoc with land use planning. Today, the city is one, but it is still differentiated by the two designations of the hilltop and the historic downtown.

Those limits of land demanded that the residents get creative with where to place the deceased. The scattered family plots that were already created would cause problems in more ways than city fathers could have ever imagined. The little burial plots that appeared sporadically over the town had to be organized and consolidated.

One advertisement posted in the *Madison Courier*, on August 20, 1849, read:

> *NOTICE*
> *The Friends of those persons buried in the private baring ground of Jesse Vauter, at North Madison will meet at the Hotel of Messrs. Branham*

& Elvin, on Thursday 30th August at 10 o'clock. A meeting to make permanent arrangements with regard to those buried there.

The first official city cemetery was located near the eastern city limits in what later came to be known as the city of Fulton, near today's Key West Shrimp House Restaurant. The restaurant's building operated at one time as a button factory, and it occupies a picturesque spot overlooking the Milton-Madison Bridge and the Ohio River. But diners seldom realize that they are just yards away from the first city cemetery. The first burial is listed as a Mrs. Slack, "In the pioneer graveyard on the bank of the town near the corner of Ferry Street in what is now Madison." That cemetery continued to be used until citizens had enough of the disturbing problem of bodies being

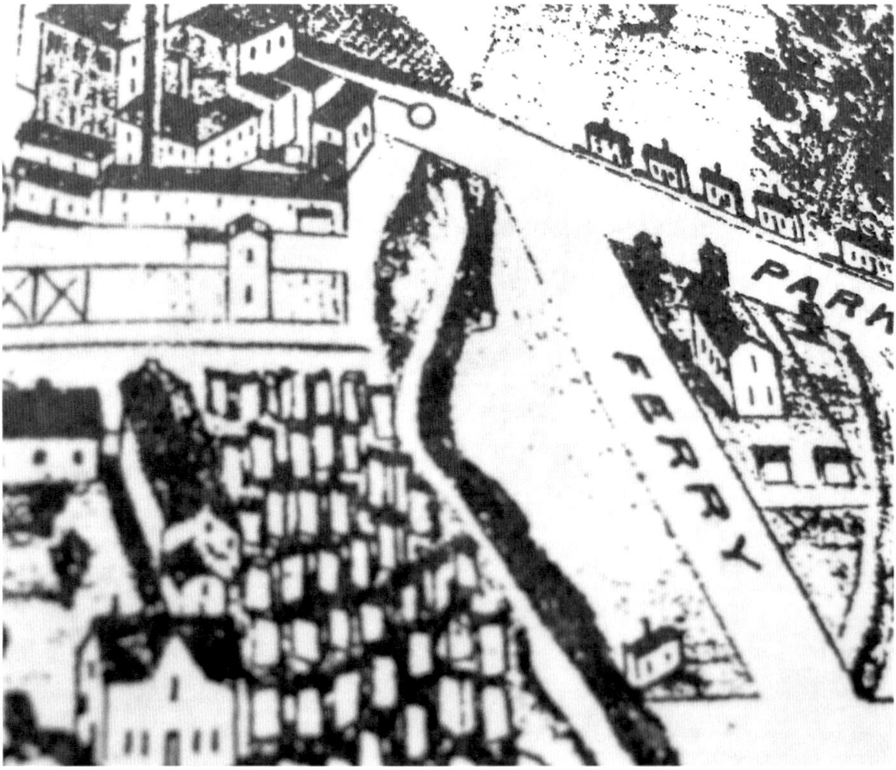

An early map of the area known as the Old City Cemetery in Fulton. Some historians say that the cemetery was probably closer to the middle of present-day Ferry Street, toward the old schoolhouse on the corner, top right. There may still be bodies in that area. 1001 Park Avenue is pictured at the top right of the picture, the last house on the left in the row of houses across from Ferry Street.

washed away during the frequent floods of the Ohio River. This is when the citizens gathered in public meetings at city hall to demand resolution of the unsettling predicament.

According to the DAR 1941 city cemetery book, Revolutionary War veteran and city founder Colonel John Paul donated land to form a new city cemetery in 1817 where today's John Paul Park is located. The cemetery began to be used as a burial ground before the declaration as the official city cemetery was issued.

One elderly resident was interviewed in 1884 by the local newspaper, which was questioning him about what he could remember of the old first cemetery. Fulton historian Vickie Young posted the account online:

> *"It is true there was an old cemetery that was destroyed, but someone remembered where it was..."*
> *...at Ferry and Lawrenceburg Road, which is now Park Avenue in Madison, Indiana, according to the Madison Courier interview of Capt. A.M. Connett, as written by Phelix Adair on December 31st 1884 for the Madison Courier (part of which read):*
>
> "Do you know where the old graveyard was located, the first one Madison ever had?"
>
> "Certainly, I do. I was present when it was wrecked. During the summer of 1839 Ferry street, the one just east of the Madison Brewing Co's establishment, was opened and graded from the river to its intersection with the Lawrenceburg road (now East Second Street) cutting through the first graveyard in Madison. A few of the graves were left, two or three, I think in the corner of the lot where the Fulton school-house now stands, and one or two on the brink of the ravine on the west side of the street. The remains taken from the other graves were all put together in a huge coffin for old Gabriel to sort out on that great day and were buried in the old cemetery on Third street. The condition of some of the remains exhumed gave rise to much speculation among the curious of that day. One coffin was found in a comparatively sound condition, but contained a lot of poplar shavings and one enough bones to construct about one-half of the human anatomy; the skull and some of the larger bones were wanting. Another, far gone in

> decay, contained the skeleton complete, but the skull was at the foot of the coffin, while the remaining portions were properly disposed. About where High street intersects Ferry street, the skeleton of an Indian chief was exhumed. He was found in a sitting posture, where the old brave had been patiently waiting to be conveyed to the happy hunting ground. A pipe, some arrow-heads and a few copper trinkets were found near the old chief's remains." Phelix Adair.

According to a family history for Andrew Jackson Grayson, "Phelix Adair" was his frequent pen name.

The process of digging up the interred to move to the new cemetery soon began. Some of the buried may not have still had family living in the area or ones who could afford the cost, and their bodies lay waiting for someone to move them to their new resting place. The second city cemetery came to be called the Third Street Cemetery and was later referred to as the Old Grave Yard. John Paul himself was buried there in 1836 and was later joined by his wife, son and daughter-in-law. The Third Street Cemetery also received bodies that had been previously resting in other locations. At least, they tried to relocate most of the bodies. There are still many times today when ground is broken during construction and bones pop up, stirred from their peaceful resting place. No wonder there are so many reports of hauntings throughout town. The rest of so many who should have been given a peaceful plot in which to spend eternity has been disturbed.

It's not known if all the bodies in the first cemetery were ever moved to Third Street. On the other hand, it appears that some were moved more than once with the relocating of the city cemetery from Third Street to Springdale Cemetery in 1859. Although this sounds barbaric today, it was often the practice to bury multiple bodies in the same coffin during times of epidemics when there was not time to individually bury the overwhelming number of poor souls who succumbed to the scourge. So we can assume that the practice was utilized when moving great numbers for reburial.

Sixty years later, there seems to be some confusion (as reported in the newspaper report on October 19, 1900) as to when the Old Grave Yard on Third Street came into use. Although this account noted that it is believed that the legal conveyance from John and Sarah Paul to the city took place in 1826, the paper was finding that many burials had taken place there before then, with the earliest it could find being recorded in 1819. Other accounts report that Captain Paul "set aside the land for burial ground in 1817." With so many different people tracking the events after the fact, it's no wonder that there are so many conflicting reports throughout all the city records. The name of a single person was recorded in the census as a George, on a deed as Gregory and as a witness as Gregor. One woman in the same family branch is listed as married to Henry by the name Daisy and then in obstetrics records as Daisy's cousin, Dora. Should we assume that the recorder knew the entire family and just became confused? Several of the records even plainly note that mistakes were made because the clerk at that time was drunk when the entry was made! Designations placed on the headstones, if there was one, were spelled exactly as written on the death certificate—"educated guesses" were necessary for some of the names.

In Madison, the same problems that had brought about the necessity to move from the first city cemetery were beginning to show up in the second city cemetery. Today, Crooked Creek still runs along the northern boundary of the property, as it did in the nineteenth century, but this was also before the creation of the runoffs designed to relieve the swelling floodwaters. Various times of the year brought about flooding, and those who should have stayed under the earth would begin to rise. Some wooden sarcophagi that had rotted away gave up their contents, with bones breaking through the ground's surface.

By 1859, the Old Third Street Cemetery had been replaced by Springdale as the official city cemetery. Springdale had been in use for twenty years by this time. This was not the only cemetery in town. In 2003, the Jefferson County Cemetery Board, which maintains old forgotten cemeteries, reported that there were 170 known cemeteries in the county, 50 of which date back to the early nineteenth century and have no one to maintain them and so are maintained by the board.

What the city did, in 1859, was pick up the headstones on Third Street on the south side of Crooked Creek and move them to Springdale on the north side of the creek toward the hill. You can see them today, lined up evenly in a row. Some were moved to other places. But like the first cemetery, we know that bodies were left behind. Some had been lost, washed away during the floods, and others may have been unknown or poor and so buried without markers. They had been laid to rest in the Third Street Cemetery—a few Revolutionary soldiers, numerous pastors and bodies of "floaters" who had been found in the Ohio River, as well as bodies of some infants, who were found in the vault and listed as "unknown." Apparently, they had been forgotten there until the mass move from those grounds. Today, the location of the vault is unknown.

The terrain that often flooded was unsuitable for building, and so the city property was reutilized and designated as a city park. The park that was created and named for the city founder, John Paul, is today the site of concerts, picnics and the occasional artistic open-air painting event. But there are also numerous reports of supernatural occurrences taking place on the grounds. Glowing orbs moving around erratically are one of the most common sightings. Crying babies are heard when none are around. Another reported sighting is an old man dressed in period clothing who walks through the park and then disappears. Likewise, an old woman was seen with a cane walking through the park as though on a Sunday walk, but she faded and then disappeared from sight.

Body Snatchers

To people of the nineteenth century, one of the most shocking practices of their day was body snatching. Many fictional accounts were based on actual events. Medical schools needed bodies to teach biological and anatomical lessons to their students, but this was a time when it was also the common belief that one needs the body to enter heaven. So, the practice was looked on with shock and indignation. It would take a pretty coarse person to enter that line of work, but there were plenty of those who would gladly dig up a freshly planted corpse for the thirty dollars that the doctors at the medical colleges paid. Those who engaged in this endeavor were called "resurrectionists."

The medical colleges had the right to utilize the bodies of unclaimed executed felons, but the limited availability opened up a whole line of work for those who had no ethics. One account reported by Janice Barnes, researcher, at the Madison–Jefferson County Library, tells of an incident involving one of the most respected doctors in the region. Dr. Charles Schussler, who at the time was president of the Madison Medical College, decided along with another local doctor, John Mullen, that it would be a grand adventure to accompany the midnight criminals on their latest excavation. Schussler's lifelong escapades are depicted in the annals of history, and his early wild experiences had prepared him to think that participating in a midnight adventure would be great fun. Janice told the tale:

> *The incident…took place on a bitterly frigid and moonless night and on this particular occasion some of the faculty decided to accompany the professionals on a procurement excursion. In the company of two resurrectionists, doctors John Mullen and Charles Schussler merrily bounced over the frozen and bumpy road as if off to a chivaree. Jovial and in high spirits they arrived at the cemetery where the two ghouls immediately set about their gruesome work. Slowly, as they waited in the stygian coldness the two doctors began to reassess the situation. Apprehension and dread crept over them and they were overcome with the gravity of their circumstances. There were stiff (no pun intended) penalties for those caught in the act of grave robbing and here they were smack in the middle of a cemetery overseeing the theft of a corpse as if they were foremen of a road gang. The ground was frozen solid and to the now edgy doctors' ears the sound of pick and shovel against the hard earth was not dissimilar to a hammer repeatedly striding an anvil. The wintry night air seemed to act as a conduit for the sound and in the doctors' minds it was amplified ten times over. The minutes seemed to drag into hours and high spirits were replaced with a high sense of alarm. In the distance a dog began to bark and a light appeared at the window of a farmhouse. The unease of the doctors and their constant prompting of speed permeated even the stoic calm of the professionals and in all haste they covered the desecrated grave and threw the frozen body into the wagon. In a great show of panic the doctors pushed and shoved and climbed over each other in order to gain position in the wagon, heedless of each other or the hapless cadaver. The driver cracked the whip and the horses lit out in a similar panic, having sensed some great distress in their passengers.*

In the haste to get away from the scene of the crime, the frozen cadaver rolled about the wagon, crashing into the crouching passengers. On one of the turns, the human icicle smashed into the foot of Dr. Schussler. In his panicked state, the pain caused him to snap, and he grabbed the head of the corpse and began banging it against the floor of the wagon, while screaming, "Hurt my foot will you!" The drivers halted the horses, and the conspirators in the wagon stared at one another until the insanity of the moment caused one and then all of the travelers to burst into bellows of laughter.

During this period, the desecration of the dead was of concern to anyone with a recently departed loved one. The poor might stand guard over a grave until it was thought to be decomposed enough to provide no use to the medical community. Those wealthy enough could have a vault of stone or brick constructed with securely locking doors. Large slabs of marble placed on top of the newly disturbed ground would also deter the removal of loved ones and inhibit the speed that the snatchers hoped for to evade detection. Some placed great iron bands around the caskets or purchased large iron cages to surround the grave site.

It would take an extraordinary event to curb the insidious yet profitable practice and encourage the enacting of severe laws. Janice went on to note that impetus, which came in 1878 when the son of President W.H. Harrison and father of U.S. senator (and later President) Benjamin Harrison, John Scott Harrison, died and was buried three days later in Ohio. Senator Harrison's son and nephew received the word that a local boy who had passed away had fallen victim to grave robbers. Finding out that he may have been taken to the Medical College of Ohio, they set out on a search. They did not find the young man, but as they were leaving, they saw the body of Senator Harrison being hoisted into the dissection room. A scandal and public outcry ensued and brought about the enactment of laws with severe penalties. The strict laws finally did their job to curb the ghoulish practice.

In Madison, the third and latest city cemetery was officially established by decree of the city council:

> *AN ORDINANCE relating to the new Burial Ground.*
>
> *Sec. 1. Be it ordained by the Common Council of the City of Madison, That the new Burial Ground north of Crooked Creek (which shall hereafter by known by the name of the Spring Dale Cemetery), be and the same is hereby opened for interments under the direction and superintendence of the Sexton.*
>
> *Sec. 2. Be it further ordained, That interments in the public part of said Cemetery shall commence on the southern extremity of parcel No. one as designed in the plan of the same, and that interments hereafter shall be regularl(y) made in each parcel, until the same be filled up. Then commencing at the southern extremity of the next parcel and so on until the same be filled to parcel No. 33.*
>
> *Sec. 3. Be it further ordained, That the parcels sold out to individuals on the eastern hill of said cemetery, or that may here after be sold, be, and the same hereby is also ready for interments.*
>
> *Sec. 4. Be it further ordained, That the Mayor is hereby authorized and permitted to sell at private sales unsold parcels appropriated for private use, at the minimum price of twenty-five dollars per each parcel, payable in six and twelve months, and that the price of the parcels heretofore sold be reduced to the above sum.*

Sec. 5. Be it further ordained, That the Mayor is hereby authorized to give to the purchaser of the above named private parcels a certificate of perpetual possession of the parcel or parcels as purchased by them, to be used solely for burial purposes.

Sec. 6. Be it further ordained, That parcels numbered from one hundred and thirty nine to one hundred and sixty, inclusive, be and the same hereby is appropriated to sale, as private parcels for the People of Color, to be sold as other private parcels by the Mayor at the minimum price of fifteen dollars each, and that parcels numbered from fifty nine to sixty four, inclusive, be appropriated as a public burying ground for the People of Color.

Sec. 7. Be it further ordained, That interments in the old burial ground be and the same hereby is prohibited, from the date hereof, unless by the special permission of the Council.

Moody Park, Mayor
Attest O.S. Pitcher Clerk,
Passed Dec. 6, 1839

The Honorable Moody Park was the first mayor of Madison, and one of the interesting dictates of this decree was that he was authorized to sell the plots in the cemetery. It is widely believed that Fannie Sullivan, "a sweet young girl" who was the fifteen-year-old daughter of Judge Jeremiah Sullivan, was the first buried at Springdale, in October 1839. Although she was probably the first buried after the decree declaring the establishment of the cemetery, there were certainly burials taking place there before then.

Mr. Grayson, the Springdale sexton, reported that there were burials in the first twenty years, a total of 3,332. For the year 1859, "The whole number of internments in Springdale was one hundred and sixty two. Of this number, seventy-one were one year old and under, ninety-eight were five years old and under, seventeen were under fifty years old, ten were sixty years and over, four were seventy years old and over and two were eighty years old. The number of internments in the same yard the previous year (1858) was one hundred and twenty five—thirty seven less than in the year just closed."

The *Madison Courier* of May 17, 1884, reported that the city was preparing to honor 193 buried soldiers for Memorial Day. At least 10 of the soldiers were listed as "unknown." One large section dedicated to the burial of Civil War soldiers is located in a highly visible area of the cemetery that interested parties can easily view.

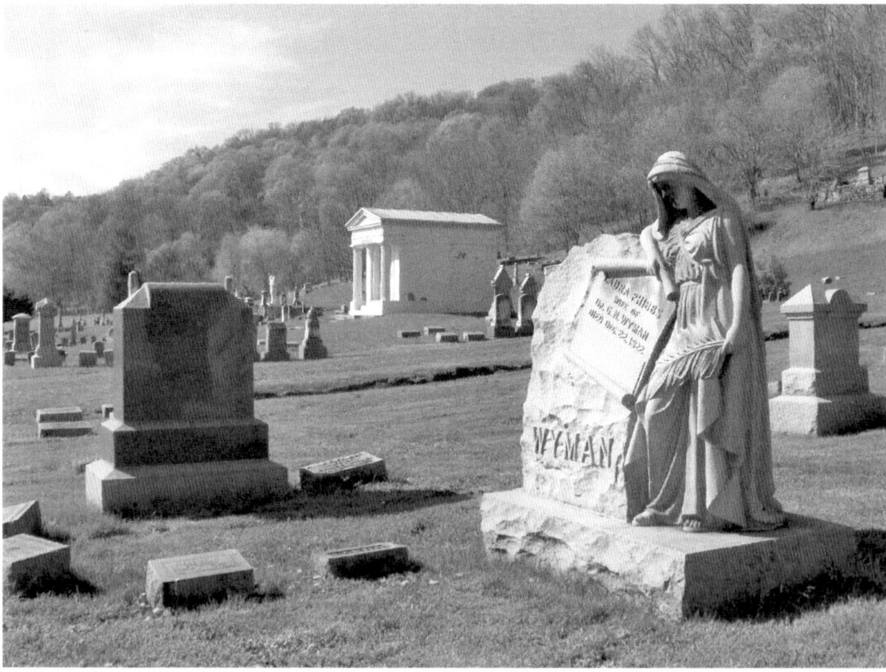

Today, Springdale Cemetery is filled with beautiful statues and, at night, numerous orbs and lost spirits.

Today, Springdale Cemetery is a working cemetery, with daily visitors and the occasional tour that informs about the old well-known Madison families buried on the grounds. Visitors often report finding unusual anomalies in their photographs. Cloud-like entities or floating orbs show up in photographs when they weren't seen in person. One old story says that on Easter morning a statue of an angel cries bloody tears. Crying babies and groans are heard by evening walkers. The forgotten dead do their best to remind the living of their certain destinies.

What to Do If You Encounter a Ghost

So many ghosts, and forms of fright,
Have started from their graves to-night,
They have driven sleep from mine eyes away;
I will go down to the chapel and pray.
—Henry Wadsworth Longfellow

Have you ever thought about what you would do if you suddenly came into contact with a ghost? It is good to be aware of what you *should* do in the case of being suddenly faced with the unexpected or if you go looking for one by "ghost hunting."

First of all, do not panic. I understand that everyone will react differently to encountering an apparition, depending on your personality and the ability to control your nerves. This is an event that most people will never experience, so try to keep your fear under control. Many who have had these encounters report that they were not afraid but rather just startled. Some may be rendered speechless, but the important thing to remember is to try to remain fairly still and observe. If you do go running from the building, don't blame yourself; it is a shock to come into contact with something that many don't even think exist. You may have some idea based on your usual reaction to sudden jolts, but you will not really know how you will react until you are actually placed in that situation.

If you can keep your wits about you and if someone else is with you, or close by, alert them to the presence. Do this calmly and try to keep them from their own sense of fear by signaling to them that it is ok. Many specters will disappear if you start to move around or if you appear to be aware of their existence. Some entities are there to communicate with you. Try to assess what this particular one is there for. Understand that if this is a residual haunting, you will not be able to interact with the spirit. It is simply energy left from another time, not an intelligent spirit that has metabolized and is there with you now.

Next, try to take into account details about the presence. You will probably tell the tale about your encounter many times over for the rest of your life, so you will want to take in all the particulars that you can at the time. Is it a full-body apparition? Is it a male or female? It's surprising, but you will probably be able to sense the gender even if it is just a shadow or a mist. Does it appear to be sad, upset or just serene? Even if there are no facial features, try to evaluate what the mood is. That way, you may be able to "help" the spirit to accomplish an undertaking that it is there to complete. Sometimes it is there to help you with some task or to tell you something. Does it seem to be unaware that it is dead? Take into account what the entity is wearing. Is it wearing a hat or clothing from another period? Does it appear in color or in shades of gray? Are there body parts missing, such as feet or an arm or the head? Missing parts may give a clue as to the cause of how a spirit left this world. How old does it appear to be? Lastly, how does the entity leave? Does it start to disappear from its head or from its feet, does it simply vanish or does it walk away through a wall or doorway?

If it so happens that you are there as part of an investigation, you may have equipment with you, like recorders, cameras or camcorders, to document any encounters. But even if this is an occurrence by chance, most people today carry cellphones that have cameras on them. If you are able to take a picture, do so. Be sure to take one after the apparition leaves to have a comparison photo.

As soon as possible after the experience, write down what you can remember. If you were with others, compare notes and ask them to write their observations down as well. What is the date and time of day that this happened? Some encounters are reported to occur on the same date for years, decades or even hundreds of years. Write down other environmental factors—was it cloudy, raining, warm or cold—and were you inside or outside? What do you think was behind the appearance? What was the overall impression that you were left with by this experience? Sometimes it is as surprised seeing you as you are at seeing it, lending credibility to the

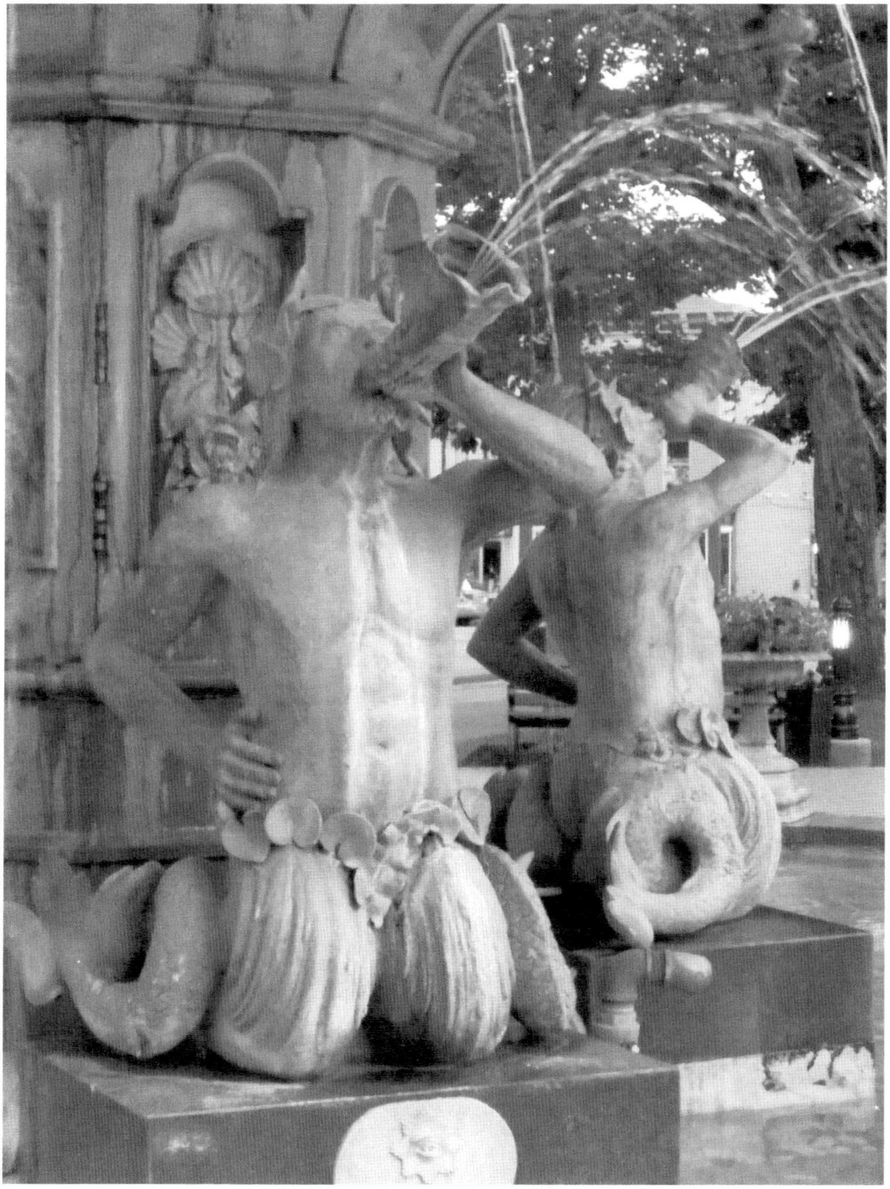

The Broadway Fountain, purchased from the 1876 Centennial Exposition in Philadelphia and donated by the Odd Fellows to the City of Madison ten years later. After its iron material became rusted from one hundred years of wear, it was restored in the 1970s with a citywide bicentennial fundraiser and was recast in bronze.

theory of other dimensions alongside this one. This may be a one-time-only happening, but ghostly appearances do tend to reoccur, so don't be surprised if it comes back. Maybe it is attracted to you or just curious about life in these times. Know that appearances are unpredictable. That is the best thing about living in this world. You just never know what to expect.

Selected Bibliography

Books

Barnes, Janice. *200 Years of Improvisation: A Book of Short Stories About Historical and Hysterical Happenings*. Madison, IN: Madison–Jefferson County Public Library, 2009.

Bruggen, Bill, and David R. Cart. *J.F.D. Lanier: America's Forgotten Patriot and Financier.* Carmel, IN: Cooper Publishing Group, 2000. Lanier Mansion Foundation.

Johnson, Doretta, with Jim Henderson. *The People in the Attic, a True Story: The Haunting of Doretta Johnson.* New York: St. Martin's Press, 1995.

Milton, John. *Paradise Lost*, 1667. Reprint, New York: Penguin Classics, 2003.

Taylor, Dave. *Murder in the House of God.* Lexington, IN: TaylorMade Write, 2008.

Van Praagh, James. *Ghosts Among Us.* New York: Harperone, 2008.

Windle, John T., and Robert M. Taylor. *The Early Architecture of Madison, Indiana.* Madison, IN: Historic Madison Inc. and the Indiana Historical Society, 1986.

Winkowski, Mary Ann. *When Ghosts Speak.* Boston, MA: Grand Central Publishing, 2007.

FILES/PAPERS

Black Files, Family History and Genealogy, Jefferson County Library.

Georgetown Historical Interpretive Walking Tour, Historic Madison Inc., 2008.

Lanier Family, Family History and Genealogy, Jefferson County Library.

Lanier Files, Jefferson County Historical Society.

Madison Cemeteries, Family History and Genealogy, Jefferson County Library.

Madison Courier, September 21, 1874.

Rea Files, Jefferson County Historical Society, Family History and Genealogy, Jefferson County Library.

Recorder's Office, Jefferson County Courthouse.

St. Patrick's Cemetery, Family History and Genealogy, Jefferson County Library.

ONLINE

Cinema Treasures. "Ohio Theater." cinematreasures.org/theaters/1663.

Ferry to Fulton. "Madison's First Cemetery." http://ferrytofulton.wordpress.com/madisons-first-cemetery.

Find-a-Grave. "Heilman." http://www.findagrave.com/cgi-bin/fg.cgi?page=gsr&GSln=Heilman&GSiman=1&GScid=86707&fb_source=message.

Jefferson County, Indiana. "Madison's First Burials—The Springdale Myth." http://jeffersoncountyindiana.blogspot.com/2008/06/madisons-first-burials-springdale-myth.html.

Renzulli, Virgil. "A Universe of at Least 10 Dimensions: String Theory Finally Reconciles Theories of Relativity and Gravity." *Columbia University Record* 23, no. 18 (March 27, 1998). http://www.columbia.edu/cu/record/23/18/14.html.

The Skeptics Dictionary. "Ouija Board." http://www.skepdic.com/ouija.html.

Stephen Wagner. http://paranormal.about.com/od/ghostsandhauntings/u/ghosts.htm.

ABOUT THE AUTHOR

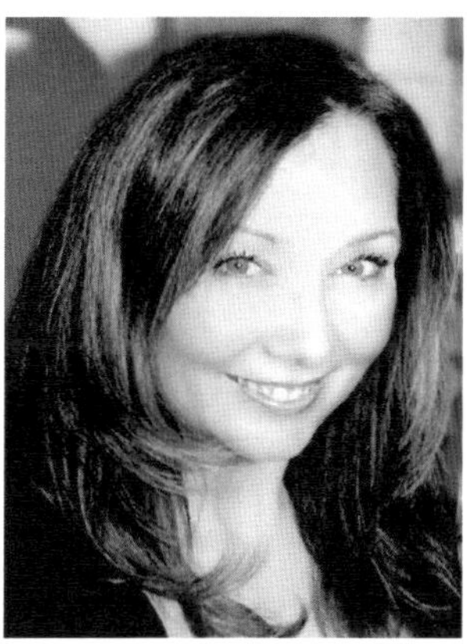

An avid preservationist, Virginia Jorgensen volunteers on local boards and leads the occasional cemetery tour. She graduated magna cum laude from Western Michigan University, where she was the recipient of the Edith Mange Award for Distinguished Scholarship in History. Mrs. Jorgensen is married to Dennis, has four children, three stepchildren, thirteen grandchildren and three pug dogs. They live in an 1848 Federal/Greek Revival home in Madison. She says, "We're not just the owners, we're the caretakers of our historic homes."

Visit us at
www.historypress.net